D1172946

More Praise for *Who's Afraid of the Big Bad Dragon?*

"Better understanding between the US and China is important not only for both nations, but for the world. Having spent the first half of his life as a student and teacher in China, and the second half as a scholar and innovator in the US, Zhao is a unique interpreter of where China's educational system has come from and where it needs to go. It should be read by caring educators around the world creating schools for the future of an uncertain world."

—MILTON CHEN, senior fellow, The George Lucas Educational Foundation; chairman, Panasonic Foundation

"Zhao's extraordinary book turns all the popular and politically hyped assumptions about East-West educational relations back to front and inside out. Asia's not an educational mirror for the West, but is actually a hall of mirrors that distorts the West's view of it. China's not an authoritative exemplar of high achievement, but is an authoritarian imposer of it. Unexpected and outrageous, this is the book that no one will ignore or want to."

—ANDY HARGREAVES, Brennan Chair of Education, Boston College; coauthor, *Uplifting Leadership*

"Yong Zhao's new work analyzes the origins, strengths, and failings of China's authoritarian education system. It is an important work—timely and concise, well-researched and well-argued—that will positively influence the debate over education reform in both the United States and in China."

—JIANG XUEQIN, Chinese education reformer; author, *Creative China*

"In *Catching Up or Leading the Way*, Zhao challenged Americans to play to their strength rather than chase the myth of foreign excellence. In *Who's Afraid of the Big Bad Dragon?*, he focuses on the US obsession with China—which he knows better than anyone writing on education policy today. Chapter 8 ("The Naked Emperor: Chinese Lessons for What Not to Do") is a devastating unmasking of the China Superiority Myth that lays responsibility at the door of PISA and lazy journalists."

—GENE V. GLASS, regents' professor emeritus, Arizona State University; research professor, University of Colorado at Boulder; coauthor, *50 Myths and Lies That Threaten America's Public Schools*

Who's AFRAID of the BIG BAD DRAGON?

Who's AFRAID of the BIG BAD DRAGON?

Why China Has the Best *(and Worst)* Education System in the World

Yong Zhao

JB JOSSEY-BASS™

A Wiley Brand

Copyright © 2014 by John Wiley & Sons, Inc. All rights reserved.

Published by Jossey-Bass
A Wiley Brand
One Montgomery Street, Suite 1200, San Francisco, CA 94104-4594
www.josseybass.com

Jossey-Bass books and products are available through most bookstores. To contact
Jossey-Bass directly call our Customer Care Department within the U.S. at 800-956-7739,
outside the U.S. at 317-572-3986, or fax 317-572-4002.

Wiley publishes in a variety of print and electronic formats and by print-on-demand.
Some material included with standard print versions of this book may not be included
in e-books or in print-on-demand. If this book refers to media such as a CD or DVD
that is not included in the version you purchased, you may download this material
at http://booksupport.wiley.com. For more information about Wiley products, visit
www.wiley.com.

**Library of Congress Cataloging-in-Publication Data has been applied for and is on file
with the Library of Congress.**

ISBN 978-1-118-48713-6 (cloth); ISBN 978-1-118-58501-6 (ebk);
ISBN 978-1-118-58491-0 (ebk)

Printed in the United States of America
FIRST EDITION
HB Printing   10 9 8 7 6 5 4 3 2 1

CONTENTS

To my parents,
who gave me the freedom to be me

ABOUT THE AUTHOR

Yong Zhao, born and raised in China's Sichuan Province, taught English in China for six years before coming to the United States as a visiting scholar in 1992. He currently holds the first Presidential Chair at the University of Oregon, where he serves as director of the Institute for Global Education and professor in the Department of Educational Measurement, Policy, and Leadership. He is also a senior fellow at the Mitchell Institute of Victoria University in Australia.

Zhao's contributions to the education field are many. He has developed computer software, including the award-winning ZON (http://enterzon.com), the world's first massively multiplayer online role-playing game for studying Chinese. The college English learning system Zhao codeveloped, New Era Interactive English, has been used by millions of college students in China since its publication in 2004. Zhao also led the development of Education for Global Citizenship, an innovative bilingual, bicultural, and dual pedagogy program for early learning. He has won numerous awards for his contributions in research, leadership, and innovation.

A popular keynote presenter, Zhao has delivered speeches and workshops in over a dozen countries on six continents. He has been quoted or featured as an expert commentator in such media outlets as *USA Today*, the *New York Times*, the *Washington*

Post, Parenting magazine, NPR, ABC, *The Australian,* Xinhua News Agency, and China's national television network, China Central TV.

Zhao is the author of more than one hundred articles and twenty books. His most recent publications include the books *Catching Up or Leading the Way: American Education in the Age of Globalization* (ASCD, 2009), *The Handbook of Asian Education* (edited; Taylor and Francis, 2011), and *World Class Learners: Educating Creative and Entrepreneurial Students* (Corwin, 2012).

ACKNOWLEDGMENTS

The Acknowledgments section is always the most difficult part of writing a book because there is no way to list all the people who have made it possible. It's especially difficult for this book due to the time it took me to complete it and the number of people from whom I have benefited.

The idea of a book about Chinese education came to me over ten years ago when I first saw the spirit of Chinese education reincarnated in the No Child Left Behind Act. Instead of writing a book about China, I ended up writing a book about education in America: *Catching Up or Leading the Way: American Education in the Age of Globalization.* I never gave up the idea of writing about the Chinese system, but it was Marjorie McAneny, my editor at Jossey-Bass, who started me on this project again. Working with Margie has been one of the most enjoyable and productive intellectual trips I have taken. Her encouraging words, gentle nudging, professional insights, and expert editing are evident in this book.

The ideas in this book are the result of numerous conversations I have had with colleagues and friends all over the world. A few individuals have significantly contributed to my thinking and deserve special recognition: Kathe Kirby, executive director of the Asia Education Foundation in Australia; Tony McKay, chair of the Australian Institute for Teaching and School Leadership; Zhong Binling, president of the China Society for Education; Gao Chen, principal of Northeast Yucai Secondary School; Gilbert Choy, founder of Beijing 3e International Kindergarten; Xuyang Yao, CEO of Beijing Channel Consulting; Sun Qijun, director of Chaoyang Education Commission in Beijing; Liu Libing, deputy director of Chaoyang Education Commission; Ron Beghetto, associate professor at the University of Connecticut; and Richard Elmore, professor at Harvard Graduate School of Education. I also thank Wanyu Xiang for her assistance with the references, particularly translating the titles of the websites referenced.

As always, my wife, Xi Chen, has been a critical and encouraging reader of the first drafts. She has also pointed me to new sources and challenged me to think and write in different ways. My son, who works at the Arts Club of Chicago, has served as an excellent example of why passion and interest matter in education. My daughter, Athena, has been a great source of inspiration and smiles.

Who's
AFRAID
of the
BIG BAD
DRAGON?

Introduction

FATAL ATTRACTION

America's Suicidal Quest for
Educational Excellence

In 2009 Beverly Hall, former superintendent of the Atlanta Public Schools, was named America's National Superintendent of the Year for "representing the 'best of the best' in public school leadership."[1] Hall was hosted in the White House by Secretary of Education Arne Duncan. In 2010, the American Educational Research Association honored her with its Distinguished Community Service Award, which "recognizes exceptional contributions to advancing the use of education research and statistics."[2] Also in 2010, President Obama appointed Hall to the elite National Board for Education Sciences.

In 2013, Hall was indicted by a grand jury in Georgia for "violation of Racketeer Influence and Corrupt Organizations Act, false statements and writings, false swearing, and theft by taking."[3] The Racketeer Influence and Corrupt Organization Act is a law typically used against Mafia leaders. If she is convicted, Hall faces forty-five years in prison.

What made Hall a national hero is precisely what brought about her downfall. She earned national recognition by significantly improving tests scores in the Atlanta Public Schools, one of America's largest urban school districts and one with a large proportion of minority students. These higher scores, it turned out, were not the result of improved student learning but of a conspiracy of teachers and school leaders. Together with Hall, thirty-four top administrators, principals, and teachers in Atlanta

High-stakes testing is America's Faustian bargain, made with the devil of authoritarianism.

were indicted for "improving" student test results through cheating. The total number of individuals involved in the scandal was even larger: some 178 principals and teachers at nearly half of Atlanta's schools were reportedly in on the scam.

This case is just one of many unfolding national scandals in the United States. Celebrated heroes have been graced with honorary titles and rewarded generous cash bonuses for dramatically improving test scores—and then exposed for cooking the books. In 2012, Lorenzo Garcia, former superintendent of the El Paso Independent School District in Texas, was sentenced to three and a half years in prison for "improving" his schools by preventing low-performing students from taking the state test. Garcia had twice been nominated for Texas Superintendent of the Year. Michelle Rhee, former chancellor of the Washington, DC, public schools, was implicated in cheating scandals soon after the district's dramatic improvement sent her to national stardom—with a prominent spot in the influential documentary *Waiting for Superman*, on the covers of *Time* and *Newsweek*, and backed with millions of dollars for her new organization StudentsFirst.

Cheating scandals have been discovered in almost every major school district that has reported great improvements: Houston, Los Angeles, Philadelphia, and New York.[4] The most obvious victims are the hundreds of thousands of innocent children directly affected by the unethical, immoral, and illegal activities of the adults working in their school systems. But millions more are affected. What about those students, teachers, and school leaders who did *not* cheat and were adversely affected by their lower test scores? Even the instigators of these cheating scandals are victims in a sense. Sure, they may have been driven by greed for the cash prizes and promotions associated with improved test scores (or by the desire to avoid punishment for reporting poor test scores). But it's unlikely that these people entered the education profession intending to hurt children for their own gains.

The villain behind these cheating scandals is the accountability system itself, which is based on high-stakes testing. Ushered in by President George W. Bush's No Child Left Behind Act in 2001 and reinforced by President Barack Obama's Race to the Top initiative in 2009, test-based accountability that directly links student performance to educators' livelihood has become the yardstick of American education. By attaching lavish rewards and harsh punishment to student test scores, the system provides powerful incentives for cheating. Educators have far less control over student performance—and far less impact on its quality—than policymakers presume. And that's especially true for teachers working in impoverished communities.

When it comes to the harm done by high-stakes testing, rampant cheating is just the tip of the iceberg. As Sharon Nichols and David Berliner point out in their book *Collateral Damage: How High-Stakes Testing Corrupts America's Schools*, this "cooking of the books" is but one of many damages done by testing reported by parents, teachers, and researchers.[5] Education historian Diane Ravitch warns in her book, *The Death and Life of the Great American School System: How Testing and Choice Are Undermining Education*, that high-stakes testing is one of the many symptoms of a virus threatening America's future.[6]

That virus is the rising tide of authoritarianism in the United States. In exchange for the comfort of knowing how their children are doing academically and that their schools are being held accountable, Americans welcomed high-stakes testing into public education. Without the benefit of historical experience with these kinds of high-stakes tests, however, Americans failed to recognize those benign-looking tests as a Trojan horse—with a dangerous ghost inside. That ghost, authoritarianism, sees education as a way to instill in all students the same knowledge and skills deemed valuable by the authority.

Despite cheating scandals and stressed-out students, America doesn't seem ready to be rid of its villain. Many Americans still believe standardized tests are needed and that problems like widespread cheating can be fixed through superficial means. Since the cheating scandals went public, most of the attention has gone to the crimes committed by a few individuals and technical fixes that would have prevented them—everything from prescribing more severe punishments to increasing testing security and inventing better tests. Political leaders have pushed aside the call to abandon high-stakes testing altogether. Secretary of Education Arne Duncan said that while he was "stunned" by the Atlanta cheating scandal, the problem "is an easy one to fix, with better test security."[7] Most parents support standardized testing and the use of test scores in teacher evaluation. Even some educators and school leaders support standardized testing, including the two largest education unions: the American Federation of Teachers and the National Education Association.

Herein lies the tragedy for America—and the reason for my writing this book.

The tale told by Chinese education illustrates the full range of tragic events that can happen under authoritarian rule. As one of the perfect incarnations of authoritarian education, China has produced superior test takers who have maintained a great civilization for millennia—but failed to cultivate talents to defend against Western aggressions backed by modern technology and sciences in the 1800s. Since that time, China has struggled to retreat from its tradition of authoritarian education. Although it has already benefited from a gradual withdrawal from central dictation, as evidenced by its recent miraculous economic growth, authoritarianism still rules.

Technical fixes won't stop the damage and embarrassment of cheating scandals. Reducing the amount of high-stakes standardized testing does little to limit its destructive influence. The damage done by authoritarianism is far greater than the instructional time taken away by testing, the narrowed educational experiences for students, and the demoralization of teachers. The deeper tragedy is the loss of values traditionally celebrated by American education—values that that helped make America the most prosperous and advanced nation in the world. Erase those values, and you lose the creative power of a culture that celebrates diversity and respects individuality. You also lose the time, resources, and opportunities you need if you are to invent a new education that will continue to lead the world.

> *The deeper tragedy is the loss of values traditionally celebrated by American education—values that that helped make America the most prosperous and advanced nation in the world.*

High-stakes testing is America's Faustian bargain, made with the devil of authoritarianism. Under the rule of authoritarianism, which gave birth to high-stakes testing in the first place, disrespect of teachers as professional colleagues and intrusion into their professional autonomy are praised as characteristics of no-nonsense, tough leadership with high expectations. Beverly Hall became national Superintendent of the Year for having "demonstrated a commitment to setting high standards for students and school personnel."[8] That commitment turned out to be authoritarian rule, as a 2012 *New York Times* report points out: "For years, Beverly L. Hall, the former school superintendent here [Atlanta schools], ruled by fear." Principals were told that if state test scores did not go up enough, they would be fired—and 90 percent of them were removed in the decade of Hall's reign. "Underlings were humiliated during rallies at the Georgia Dome," to set an example of Hall's "rule by fear," the *New York Times* report continues. "Dr. Hall permitted principals with the highest test scores to sit up front near her, while sticking those with the lowest scores off to the side, in the bleachers." Moreover, "she was chauffeured around the city, often with an entourage of aides and security guards. When she spoke publicly, questions had to be submitted beforehand for screening."[9]

Lorenzo Garcia, the former El Paso superintendent, was another action-oriented leader praised for his miracles. He kept almost half of students eligible for tenth grade from taking the tenth-grade exam by not allowing them to enroll in the school, retaining them at ninth grade, or rushing them into eleventh grade. Although what he did was reported and investigated by both the US Department of Education and the Texas Education Agency, twice he got away "because he held people's careers in his hands....If you said no to him, you were gone," said El Paso's director of student services, Mark Emmanuel Mendoza on NPR.[10] El Paso has a large population of Mexican immigrants, and Garcia also exploited the community's fear of the courts, fear of the Border Patrol, and trust in the school system. The students excluded from the tenth-grade exam "were made to feel like they did something wrong," said Linda Romero, the drop-out prevention counselor who blew the whistle.[11]

Under the spell of authoritarianism, the Obama administration has consistently disregarded the law, not to mention the checks and balances of American democracy. Instead of reworking the expired No Child Left Behind Act, President Obama and his secretary of education have given out waivers to states, exempting them from the law in exchange for their willingness to accept the administration's wishes. States have responded favorably, and

Congress has largely forgiven, if not condoned, the administrations' actions.

Under the spell of authoritarianism, 50 million American children are being taught a de facto national curriculum, then subjected to a de facto national standardized test. The Common Core State Standards Initiative, created with little input from the people or their representatives, is now enforced with tax dollars in nearly all states. Although the federal government did not technically pay for its development or officially adopt its standards, the billions of dollars in the Race to the Top program, which required the adoption of common standards and assessment, undoubtedly helped the CCSS spread.

Under the spell of authoritarianism, Americans have willingly surrendered their beloved local governments to state and federal control. Locally elected school boards have turned into bureaucratic branches of state and federal government, for in effect, they only collect local taxes. They then use that tax money to implement the wishes of the state and federal governments in curriculum, pedagogy, and assessment.

Authoritarianism has driven America to admire, glorify, and emulate other authoritarian education systems because they seem to produce "results," defined as test scores. Instead of valuing what their own educational methods can produce, American leaders envy countries with top test scores in a narrow set of subjects—which is simply a sign of how successfully those countries have homogenized their

> *American leaders envy countries with top test scores in a narrow set of subjects—which is simply a sign of how successfully those countries have homogenized their students.*

students. Mistaking China's miseries as secrets to success, American education pundits and political leaders have been eager to learn from the quintessential authoritarian education system. Ironically, they've condemned China's authoritarian political system in the same breath.

A survival strategy the Chinese people developed to cope with thousands of years of authoritarian rule has been glorified as China's secret to educational success. The belief that the Chinese attach high values to education is widespread in the United States.[12] That belief has been used to explain the educational success of Chinese students; it has also been used to condemn Americans in general, and some racial and cultural groups in particular, for their poor test scores.

This belief is, however, an illusion at best and a cruel glorification of authoritarianism at worst. The Chinese people were deprived of any other means to succeed in life, both spiritually and materially. Their only option was to pass the exams dictated by the absolute authority—emperors in the past and the government today. When people are convinced that there are no worthy options to pursue in life except the narrow path prescribed by an authoritarian government, they are forced to comply, accept indoctrination, and be homogenized. For this reason, Chinese parents have to invest generously in their children's education and test preparation; their efforts mitigate the lack of sufficient investment from the government. When onlookers praise the efficiency of the Chinese educational system, in which minimal government investment begets huge gains in test scores, they ignore the resources Chinese parents throw into the pot.

The Chinese have also been praised for emphasizing effort and diligence instead of inherent intelligence or social conditions. Again, this is no more than a mistaken romanticization of an authoritarian ploy to deny the existence of individual differences and unequal social conditions. Emphasizing effort is a convenient way for the authority to evade responsibility for leveling the playing field for those with diverse abilities and talents. It is an excuse for not providing programs for children with disabilities or those born into extremely unfavorable social circumstances. It also serves as a seductive marketing slogan, persuading individuals to welcome homogenization.

Admirers also glorify Chinese students' inability to question and challenge authority. For instance, Andreas Schleicher, in defending China's top PISA ranking, noted how much more likely Chinese students are to blame themselves instead of their teachers for their failure in math, compared to their counterparts in France.[13] While the finding is correct, Schleicher fails to notice its cause: an authoritarian culture that tends to shift the blame from the authority, which no one dares to question, to the students. This is true in other authoritarian education systems as well; just look at Russia, Indonesia, and Singapore.

The Chinese national educational system has won high praise as an efficient system with national standards, a national curriculum, a high-stakes test (the college entrance exam), and a clearly defined set of gateways to mark students' transitions from one stage to another.[14] Admirers note that every Chinese student has a clear and focused goal to pursue; Chinese teachers and parents know exactly what to do to help their students; and the government knows exactly which schools are doing well. What those admirers ignore is the fact that such an education system, while being an effective machine to instill what the government wants students to learn, is incapable of supporting individual strengths, cultivating a diversity of talents, and fostering the capacity and confidence to create.

I wrote this book to show how China, a perfect incarnation of authoritarian education, has produced the world's best test scores at the cost of diverse, creative, and innovative talents. I also tried to illustrate how difficult it is to move away from authoritarian thinking by showing how China has struggled to reform its education for over a century. The book is intended to warn the United

States and other Western countries about the dangerous consequences of educational authoritarianism.

Education in the West must go through transformative changes. A paradigm shift will be necessary if we are to prepare children to live successfully in the new world: a shift I wrote about in my previous book, *World Class Learners; Educating Creative and Entrepreneurial Students*.[15] As traditional routine jobs are offshored and automated, we need more and more globally competent, creative, innovative, entrepreneurial citizens—job creators instead of employment-minded job seekers. To cultivate new talents, we need an education that enhances individual strengths, follows children's passions, and fosters their social-emotional development. We do *not* need an authoritarian education that aims to fix children's deficits according to externally prescribed standards.

> *If the United States and the rest of the West are concerned about being overtaken by China, the best solution is to avoid becoming China.*

If the United States and the rest of the West are concerned about being overtaken by China, the best solution is to avoid becoming China. The empire that led the world for over two millennia was shattered by Western technological and scientific innovations in the 1800s. Its education represents the best of the past. It worked extremely well for China's imperial rulers for over one thousand years, but it stopped working when the modern world emerged. The Chinese system continued to produce students who excel in a narrow range of subjects. Only 10 percent of its college graduates are deemed employable by multinational businesses because these students lack the very qualities our new society needs.[16]

China's achievements over the past thirty years should be no reason for the United States and other Western nations to panic, as forewarned by French historian Nicolas Boulanger more than 250 years ago: "All the remains of her ancient institutions, which China now possesses, will necessarily be lost; they will disappear in the future revolutions; as what she hath already lost of them vanished in former ones; and finally, as she acquires nothing new, she will always be on the losing side."[17]

Discussion questions for each chapter are available. Register at www.wiley.com/go/dragon using the password 87136.

1

FOOLING CHINA, FOOLING THE WORLD

Illusions of Excellence

O ne hundred years ago, a Columbia University law professor
named Frank Johnson Goodnow was dispatched to China
to help design the nation's new government. Goodnow would
find both irony and vindication in the West's idolization and envy
of China today.

In 1911, a revolution led by Dr. Sun Yat-sen had ended two
thousand years of imperial rule and established China as a republic.[1] Sun had been elected provisional president, but he gave up
the position to Yuan Shikai, a military leader who forced the last
emperor to abdicate his throne in 1912.

China needed a constitution.

Acting on the suggestion of Charles Eliot, president emeritus
of Harvard and a trustee of the Carnegie Endowment for
International Peace, the Chinese government sought out an
expert to help draft its governing principles. Goodnow was
selected from several candidates and appointed for a three-year
term, with an annual salary of $12,000. On May 3, 1913, he arrived
in Beijing. Although his duties were merely advisory and he left
China the following year to assume the presidency of Johns
Hopkins University, he developed two drafts—one in 1913, while
in China, and another in 1915, after his departure.

The essence of his first draft made it into the provisional constitution that went into effect in May 1914. Called the "Goodnow
Constitution," it gave the nation's president unchecked power

over Chinese citizens, "foreign affairs, war and peace, appointment and removal of officials, and budget and financial matters."[2] The second version, based on Goodnow's 1915 memorandum, would have made Yuan Shikai practically the emperor had he not died in 1916.

Goodnow became known as the "embarrassed monarchist"; he was sharply criticized for ending China's young democracy. A *Baltimore Evening Sun* cartoon portrayed him as a carpenter helping President Yuan tear down the infant republic and restore imperial rule. He "came to be remembered as the foreign stooge of a Chinese dictator."[3] Goodnow and his defenders claimed that he'd been manipulated, his words used selectively by President Yuan and his supporters. Nonetheless, Goodnow still maintained that "a monarchy is better suited than a republic to China" for reasons of stability and efficiency. He didn't think China was ready for popular self-government: "Chinese society is so unorganized and so unconscious of any common interests, that it is almost impossible to start parliamentary government here, as we started it in England, on the foundation of economic or social interest."[4] Instead of a powerful parliament, he said, "China required a stable, permanent government and a powerful, independent president."[5]

> *The People's Republic has all the features of Goodnow's ideal government: it is powerful, stable, permanent, and independent, without any significant, meaningful influence from the people.*

A century has since passed, and China has reinvented itself several times. When the Communists rose to power, the original Republic of China retreated to the island of Taiwan, where it is considered a province. The Communist government gained control over the vast majority of China and established the People's Republic of China (PRC) in 1949. Taiwan evolved into a multiparty democracy; the PRC remained a single-party (Communist) government. Although today's China—that is, the People's Republic of China—is not the monarchy Goodnow suggested, its essence is absolute monarchist. There's only one essential difference: the monarch is not a person but a party. The People's Republic has all the features of Goodnow's ideal government: it is powerful, stable, permanent, and independent, without any significant, meaningful influence from the people.

Given the negative response he received at the time, Frank Goodnow couldn't possibly have imagined today's growing admiration for the authoritarian government he suggested for China. Yet that government has been praised not only for leading China's miraculous economic growth and making it the world's second largest economy, but also for providing a viable alternative to the model of development in the dominant Western-style democracies.[6] What would be even harder for Goodnow to imagine? The fact that there are now US citizens eager to import the Chinese style of government to America.

"CHINA FOR A DAY"

Thomas Friedman, the influential *New York Times* columnist who has written several best sellers on global issues, just might be China's biggest fan. More than once, he has expressed a "fantasy" of America being China for a day. The notion first appeared as the title of a chapter in his 2008 book *Hot, Flat, and Crowded: Why We Need a Green Revolution—and How It Can Renew America*. He then repeated his China-for-a-day dream on NBC's *Meet the Press* in May 2010, telling host David Gregory, "I have fantasized—don't get me wrong—but that what if we could just be China for a day?"[7]

Friedman believes a Chinese-style government offers great efficiency—the exact point Goodnow used to support his monarchy proposal a century ago. Frustrated with the ineffectual American government and its tedious two-party wrangling, Friedman wants a "China day" when "we could actually, you know, authorize the right solutions, and I do think there is a sense of that, on, on everything from the economy to environment."[8] In a 2009 *New York Times* column, he explains why the authoritarian Chinese style government is better than American democracy: "One-party autocracy certainly has its drawbacks. But when it is led by a reasonably enlightened group of people, as China is today, it can also have great advantages. That one party can just impose the politically difficult but critically important policies needed to move a society forward in the 21st century."[9]

Would Goodnow agree? He suggested an authoritarian government for China a century ago on the grounds that it wasn't yet ready for a popular democracy. But Friedman seems to view an authoritarian government as inherently preferable to a popular democracy. And unlike Goodnow, who based his suggestion on a series of logical assumptions, Friedman claims to have empirical evidence. In his latest three books—including *That Used to Be Us: How America Fell Behind in the World It Invented and How We Can Come Back*—Friedman offers statistics, anecdotes, personal observations, and interviews that relate the great achievements of China's forward-looking, visionary, courageous, wise, powerful, benevolent—and authoritarian—leadership.[10]

After all, in merely thirty years, China's gross domestic product, a measure of the total size of a nation's economy, expanded thirty-fold, from $202 billion in 1980 to over $7 trillion in 2011. In 2007, China surpassed Germany to become the world's third largest economy.[11] Three years later, China replaced Japan as the world's second largest economy.[12] It is now well on the way to becoming the world's largest economy. Estimates vary, but China is generally projected to overtake the United States and become number one in the next decade.[13]

In 2008, China dazzled the world with the Summer Olympic Games. The awe-inspiring opening ceremony, the guaranteed blue skies, the long list of foreign dignitaries, and the grand facilities drove home a single message: China had become a powerful player on the world stage. The 2010 World Expo, with over 250 countries participating, was another extravagant event that showed off a transformed and modernized China. China now has the world's longest high-speed rail, a third of the world's one hundred tallest buildings, and a network of expressways larger than the United States. It even (temporarily) took the title of the fastest computer away from the United States.

"THE BEIJING CONSENSUS"

Thomas Friedman isn't the only one to notice China's astonishing growth and attribute it to a superior system of economic development. In 2004, Joshua Cooper Ramo, a former senior and foreign editor of *Time* magazine, published a seminal paper, "The Beijing Consensus,"[14] through the UK-based Foreign Policy Center. A journalist and consultant, Ramo has extensive experiences with China. He based his findings on "more than 100 off-the-record discussions with leading thinkers in Chinese universities, think tanks and government." [15]

Ramo coined the term *Beijing consensus* in pointed contrast to *Washington consensus*, a neoliberal and market-fundamentalist perspective for economic development derived from the Western liberal democratic tradition. Ramo wanted to show that "China is in the process of building the greatest asymmetric superpower the world has ever seen."[16] He believes that "China is marking a path for other nations around the world who are trying to figure out not simply how to develop their countries, but also how to fit into the international order in a way that allows them to be truly independent, to protect their way of life and political choices in a world with a single massively powerful centre of gravity. The Beijing consensus, he argues, "replaces the widely-discredited Washington Consensus, an economic theory made famous in the 1990s for its prescriptive, Washington-knows-best approach to telling other nations how to run themselves."[17]

A slew of publications followed describing China's rise as a global power that has begun to shape a new world order. Major media outlets in the West began assigning stories about China's growing global influence. A 2007 *Time* magazine article, "China Takes on the World," asserted that "through its foreign investments and appetite for raw materials, the world's most populous country has already transformed economies from Angola to Australia. Now China is turning that commercial might into real political muscle, striding onto the global stage and acting like a nation that very much intends to become the world's next great power."[18]

In 2008 Joshua Kurlantzick, a special correspondent for the *New Republic* and visiting scholar at the Carnegie Endowment for International Peace, published *Charm Offensive: How China's Soft Power Is Transforming the World.*[19] "Soft power" is a designation first used by Harvard political scientist Joseph S. Nye Jr. in his 2004 book, *Soft Power: The Means to Success in World Politics.*[20] In contrast to hard power—the ability to coerce—soft power is the ability to attract and persuade. Hard power comes from a country's military or economic strength, while soft power lies in the attractiveness of a country's culture, political ideals, and policies.

The year 2009 brought another best seller about the superior Chinese way: *When China Rules the World: The End of the Western World and the Birth of a New Global Order* by the British journalist Martin Jacques.[21] He too admired China's recent growth, then went a few steps further, describing how China had found its way to modernity without being Westernized and predicting that the

Chinese way will become the more successful system in the future. China's rise, predicted Jacques, will end Western domination.

Following Jacques's line of argument, Stefan Halper, director of American studies at the University of Cambridge, put forth more evidence that China's autocratic leadership has worked well and will continue to do so domestically and internationally. In his 2012 book, *The Beijing Consensus: Legitimizing Authoritarianism in Our Time*, he argues that while the US democratic government seems to hinder its economic progress, China's autocratic leadership is laying a foundation for future economic success.[22] Joshua Kurlantzick echoes Halper in his 2013 book, *Democracy in Retreat: The Revolt of the Middle Class and the Worldwide Decline of Representative Government*:

> Today, China—and to a lesser extent other successful authoritarian capitalists—offer a viable alternative to the leading democracies. In many ways, their systems pose the most serious challenge to democratic capitalism since the rise of communism and fascism in the 1920s and early 1930s. And in the wake of the global economic crisis, and the dissatisfaction with democracy in many developing nations, leaders in Asia, Africa, and Latin America are studying the Chinese model far more closely—a model that, eventually, will help undermine democracy in their countries.[23]

"SURPASSING SHANGHAI"

While China's authoritarian capitalism is held up as a model for developing countries, China's educational system is downright worshipped, even in the developed West. Thomas Friedman wants America to be China only "for a day" politically, but when it comes to education, a growing number of Western political leaders, academics, school reformers, and media pundits want to be China forever. And although it's unlikely, setting aside Friedman's fantasy, that any Western democratic nation will seriously borrow

Thomas Friedman only wants America to be China "for a day," but a growing number of Western political leaders, academics, school reformers, and media pundits want to be China forever.

China's form of government any time soon, it's already the aspiration of many Western nations to outeducate China, and to do it in the Chinese way.

For an example, read *Surpassing Shanghai: An Agenda for American Education Built on the World's Leading Systems*.[24] Marc Tucker, CEO of the National Center for Education and the Economy (NCEE), pulled together NCEE research to analyze the five leading education systems in the world: Finland, Japan, Singapore, Canada (Ontario), and Shanghai, chosen to represent China. Shanghai earned its place primarily because of its students' scores on the Program for International Student Assessment (PISA). PISA, coordinated by the Paris-based Organization for Economic Cooperation and Development, measures fifteen-year-old students' reading, mathematics, and science literacy. Given every three years since 2000, it has become the world's largest international educational assessment, with some seventy countries participating in the 2009 round—Shanghai's first. It was the first time any Chinese students had taken the PISA or any other large-scale international assessment. The Shanghai students aced the test, scoring top in all three categories, and they did it again in the 2012 round.

The sweep shouldn't have been surprising: Chinese students have been outscoring their counterparts in the United States and other Western countries in smaller-scale comparative studies for quite a long time. Two decades ago, *The Learning Gap: Why Our Schools Are Failing and What We Can Learn from Japanese and Chinese*

Education, coauthored by psychologists Harold Stevenson and James Stigler, systematically documented the superb performance of Chinese students and the characteristics of their outstanding education.[25] But the PISA results officially earned China the "world's best education" title, and that victory had a powerful effect on the West. The *New York Times* reported that the Chinese students' performance had "stunned" American experts and political leaders.[26] "An absolute wake-up call" to US Secretary of Education Arne Duncan, it gave President Obama a "Sputnik moment," suggesting that China had beaten America in education just as the former Soviet Union had beaten America into space. Ever since the 2009 PISA results came out, Obama has repeatedly vowed to outeducate China in order to outcompete it.

Shanghai is China's most sophisticated urban center. Perhaps its students' results were an exception? In 2012, students from nine Chinese provinces took the test. PISA chief Andreas Schleicher, the German statistician who managed to rebrand the test as the gold standard of education, hinted to BBC reporter Sean Coughlan about the unpublished results: "Shanghai is an exceptional case—and the results there are close to what I expected. But what surprised me more were the results from poor provinces that came out really well. The levels of resilience are just incredible." Coughlan's article, titled "China: The World's Most Clever Country?" summed up Schleicher's praise for Chinese education: not only would the test results for disadvantaged pupils be the envy of any Western country, but taken as a whole, "the findings indicate that China has an education system that is overtaking many Western countries."[27]

Such a great education is certainly worth emulating, especially for Western countries convinced they're losing their battle with China on the education front. In December 2010, shortly after visiting China, British Secretary of Education Michael Gove published a passionate commentary in the *Telegraph.*[28] He recounted his amazement when he was given a book of published research papers, all written by students in a Beijing school. "Schools in the Far East are turning out students who are working at an altogether higher level than our own," Gove wrote, urging his country "to implement a cultural revolution just like the one they've had in China." At the close of his commentary, he announced, "Like Chairman Mao, we've embarked on a Long March to reform our education system."

Gove devised a long list of revolutionary strategies, like lengthening school days and shortening holidays for British children. In April 2013, he announced his proposal, and he won strong support from the Whitehall with yet another reminder: "We can either start working as hard as the Chinese, or we'll all soon be working for the Chinese."[29]

The message to the Brits: do as the Chinese do or else risk being taken over. John Holdren, director of the White House Office of Science and Technology Policy, told the UK newspaper the *Independent* in 2011: "Everybody is looking at China and saying, if we don't lift our game, China is going to eat our lunch economically."[30]

"BE AFRAID OF THE FRIENDS WHO FLATTER YOU"

China's recent accomplishments certainly deserve to be recognized, and China is of course happy to have its triumphs acknowledged by outsiders. As the oldest continuous civilization, China suffered humiliating defeats by Western powers in the 1800s, and for nearly two hundred years, it was left far behind. The Chinese economy stagnated. Chinese immigrants were mistreated and excluded from the mainstream in many Western countries. The underpinning values of the Chinese culture were called into question again and again by both the Chinese and Westerners.

Since the 1800s, outside forces have tried using religious, economic, military, and political forces to Westernize China—all without much success. Until very recently, the West was trying to export its cultural and ideological values, its Christianity, and its economic and political system to China. Now, all of a sudden, China has been pronounced the model for others because of its superior political system, education, and culture. And those "others" include influential Westerners.

Not surprisingly, the West's praise has been received hungrily by China, a country that has yearned for outside recognition for a long time. Compliments are warmly welcomed by the Chinese government, which is eager for any evidence to ensure its legitimacy. Publications praising China are quickly translated and published in China, where they become instant best sellers. Authors such as Thomas Friedman and Martin Jacques are China's close friends and honored guests, treated as royalty by government officials and nationalistic media.

But questioning voices have begun to emerge. Bold Chinese scholars caution the Chinese not to be "murdered by flattery" from Western writers. In *China Refuses to Be Killed by Flattery*, Shu Taifeng, an editor of *Oriental Perspectives* (a popular Chinese news magazine similar to *Time* or *Newsweek*), explains why China should be cautious:

> Why is it a bad thing to be praised? It seems to be a silly question. However, if the people who praise you do not really understand you, this flattery is either the result of general good intentions or romantic idolization as a form of self-motivation. Or it could be that they want something from you, even to lure you to sacrifice yourself for them...

> Praising China has become a fashionable trend both within and without China. Their motivation varies, but regardless, "the tree wants to remain calm although the wind does not stop." If China does not stay calm, we will lose our cool head before these sincere and not so sincere praises and lose our orientation. If so, flattery becomes murderous.

Our neighbor Japan has been "murdered by flattery." Japan grew tremendously after the Second World War and rebuilt itself as a powerful economy in about 20 years. Western praise for Japan at the time was not a little bit less than today's flattery of China. The American scholar Ezra Vogel published *Japan as Number One: Lessons for America* in 1979, suggesting that Japan had surpassed the U.S. in many aspects. Nevertheless, in less than 10 years, Japan's economic bubble burst and has slipped into decades of recession.[31]

"A VERY LARGE GAP"

Chinese leaders and scholars are keenly aware of the issues China faces. "China has increased its competitiveness in some areas, but there is a very large gap between China and developed countries," said Yang Jiechi, China's minister of foreign affairs, in his opening remarks at the 2013 US-China Strategic and Economic Dialogue.[32] In his book, Shu cites abundant data to show that despite three decades of stunning growth, China's economy remains volatile, not only because it has a fragile foundation with extremely low per capita wealth but also because of structural imbalances characterized by growing income inequality, increasing mass protests, a deteriorating environment, and lagging development of "soft power." "An even more important and perhaps key challenge is the decoupling of political and economic reforms," Shu writes, "even the direction of reforms is still fuzzy." Burdened with massive challenges, Shu pleads with the Chinese to remain "calm, calm, and calm" and not be fooled by Western authors such as Martin Jaques, who have a very "shallow" understanding of China.

Shu Taifeng is not alone. His book has been well received and hotly discussed inside China. In spite of its apparently negative views of China, a state-controlled publishing house published it. It was also carried online by multiple online portals under close watch of the government. Even state-run media outlets have run opinion pieces echoing Shu's views.

Although the political system is an extremely sensitive subject in China—and debate about it is generally silenced—education is discussed pretty freely. Again, although the Chinese are happy that their students scored higher than everyone else in the world, virtually no one in China believes that the country has the best education system. The Chinese government has undertaken numerous massive efforts to reform public education. Chinese parents have spent their life savings to send their children to study overseas or in Western-style schools in China rather than keep them in the "world's best education system." Education has been widely recognized as the primary culprit for China's lack of creative and innovative talents—and a major concern for China's success in the future.

FATAL ATTRACTION: THE REAL CHINA THREAT

The West has dominated the world for two centuries, with Britain owning the nineteenth century and the United States the twentieth. At the moment it looks as if China will reign in the twenty-first century—an intensely uncomfortable prospect for America and other Western countries. According to a 2012 Pew Research Center survey, 52 percent of the general public in the United States were concerned that "China's emergence as a world power is a major threat to the U.S."[33] See figures 1.1 and 1.2.

While some are concerned about China's military power, more are worried about its economic prowess. The Pew survey found that 59 percent of Americans were concerned about China's economic strength compared to 28 percent concerned about its military strength. A majority (62 percent) of Americans viewed China as a competitor. Majorities were worried about China holding large amounts of American debt (78 percent), taking away US jobs (71 percent), and causing the large trade deficit to the United States (61 percent).

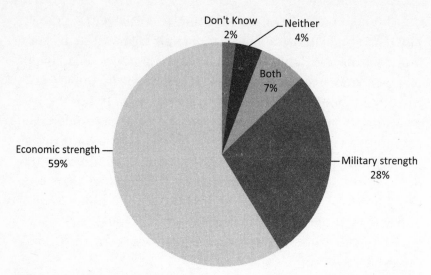

Figure 1.1   Percentage of Americans Who Are Concerned about China's Military and Economic Strength
Source: "US Public, Experts Differ on China Policies," Pew Research Center, Washington, DC. September 18, 2012, http://www.pewglobal.org/files/2012/09/US-Public-and-Elite-Report-FINAL-FOR-PRINT-September-18-2012.pdf. Reprinted with permission.

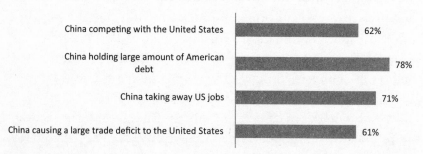

Figure 1.2   What Worries Americans the Most about China's Economy
Source: "US Public, Experts Differ on China Policies," Pew Research Center, Washington, DC. September 18, 2012, http://www.pewglobal.org/files/2012/09/US-Public-and-Elite-Report-FINAL-FOR-PRINT-September-18-2012.pdf. Reprinted with permission.

Until recently, most Westerners haven't been concerned about the existential threat the China model presents to the West. But the more we glorify China as a viable model of economic development, the more anxiety Westerners will feel about China's political influence on the global stage. In his article, "How China Will Change the Global Political Map," Martin Jacques makes this prediction:

> China has the world's second largest economy. As it overtakes the United States in the relatively near future, and becomes the world's largest economy, China will exercise a growing global influence. Meanwhile, the West—the home of Western liberal democracy—is in relative economic decline. By 2030, it will, by one estimate, account for only 28 percent of global GDP, compared with 33 percent for China and 67 percent for the developing world. In such circumstances, the West's political influence is bound to decline.[34]

Despite widespread concerns about China's rise, it is unlikely that China will invade any other country, let alone engage in military conflicts with the West. As the Harvard political scientist Joseph Nye Jr. wrote recently, "Given shared global challenges like financial stability, cybercrime, nuclear proliferation, and climate change, China and the United States also have much to gain from working together."[35] The economic threat is also debatable. Some economists would argue that China may have brought more economic benefits than threats to the United States and the West by opening its vast market, supplying inexpensive labor, and making stabilizing investments during times of economic turmoil. Although it is painful to see jobs lost to China, this is the nature of economic development, and such offshoring brings stimuli for new innovations and new industries. The political threat may have been grossly exaggerated as well. China, according to many analysts, is not going to take over the United States any time soon. "Right now, the United States is vastly more powerful than the

People's Republic of China," wrote Daniel W. Drezner, professor of international politics at Tufts University. "Anyone telling you otherwise is selling you something."[36]

China does present a dangerous threat. That threat, however, does not originate with China or its actions. The threat comes from the West's current infatuation with China's educational system and from the actions that countries such as the United States and Great Britain have taken to emulate that system. Those actions betray a shallow understanding of a very old and complex culture, and they confuse short-term outcomes with long-term, sustainable progress.

Chinese education is authoritarian in nature, and it has been for centuries. The spirit of education in China today flows from a two-thousand-year history of imperial exams. Chinese education produces excellent test scores, a short-term outcome that can be achieved by rote memorization and hard work, but like the Chinese government itself, it does not produce a citizenry of diverse, creative, and innovative talent. Chinese education proved a failure back in 1842, when China lost the first Opium War to Great Britain. Ever since then, China has been trying to learn from the West.

If Western countries successfully adopt China's education model and abandon their own tradition of education, they may see their standing rise on international tests, but they will lose what has made them modern: creativity, entrepreneurship, and a genuine diversity of talents.

The only way China will win the global competition of the future is for the West to begin educating the way China does.

2

THE EMPERORS' GAME

A Perfect Machine for Homogenization

When we admire Chinese education today, we're admiring essentially the same characteristics that infatuated Europeans in the seventeenth and eighteenth centuries. Gottfried Wilhelm Liebniz, for example, the brilliant German Lutheran philosopher and mathematician, had a love for the Chinese polity and philosophy that rivals any expressed today. "Even if we are equal to them in the productive arts, and...in the theoretical sciences," he wrote, "it is certainly true (I am almost ashamed to admit) that they surpass in practical philosophy, by which I mean the rules of ethics and politics which have been devised for the conduct and benefit of human life."[1]

Jesuit missionaries to China shared the same opinion, sending glowing stories back to Europe about the Oriental Empire's superior Confucian philosophy and utopian society. Their observations so challenged Christian orthodoxy that several books on China were ordered burned by the church, including *Nouveau mémoire sur l'état présent de la Chine* by Father Louis le Comte. The French Jesuit missionary dared to assert that the Chinese system of morality was "on a par with the Christian revelation as a supreme product of the moral aspirations of Man."[2] And the German philosopher Christian Wolff was ordered to leave his position at the University of Halle immediately after delivering a speech expressing his admiration for China: "In the Art of Governing, this Nation has even surpassed all others without exception."[3]

Bonfires and dismissals did not prevent China from becoming, in Europe, "better known than some provinces of Europe itself." Sinophilism swiftly developed into Sinomania.[4] The French Enlightenment writer François-Marie Arouet, better known as Voltaire, was among the most devoted Sinophiles, along with the French economist François Quesnay, who was dubbed the "Confucius of Europe."[5] Both Voltaire and Quesnay fell in love with Chinese despotism and suggested that it be a model for European nations. China's political system struck Voltaire as ideal: "the combination of a monarch with almost unlimited powers and an official class chosen on a rational, that is on an intellectual, basis, and noteworthy for its freedom from political corruption as well as from religious bias."[6]

Westerners were awed by the strengths of China's official class. Sinologist A. R. Davis, of the University of Sydney, writes about "the Chinese scholar-official" and makes "little apology for this somewhat cumbersome term, because, if he were an object of wonder to the Western world, it is hardly surprising that our Western vocabulary should lack a satisfactory equivalent." The labels "literati," "bureaucrats," "mandarins," and "gentry" are all inaccurate "for it was because scholars were the officials and the officials were scholars that Voltaire admired China's government."[7] The Chinese scholar-officials have been held in high esteem for centuries, praised for making China the prosperous and stable empire it was. First, they occupied government positions, administering the daily business of the government on behalf of the emperor, the Son of Heaven. On retirement, they served as moral examples, teachers, and unofficial judges. They didn't simply carry out the orders of the rulers; they guided the rulers. Kenneth Winston, lecturer in ethics at Harvard Kennedy School of Government, wrote a paper in 2005 suggesting "that only by integrating the technocratic aspects of a Kennedy School of Government education with the ethical orientation of scholar-officials can the Chinese provide for the requisites of public administration in a future democratic society."[8] Winston describes the scholar-officials as

> a self-conscious, educated elite who took it as their highest calling to enter government service, typically in the central bureaucracy or in provincial administrations. As humanists steeped in the moral wisdom of the past (i.e. the classic Confucian texts), they devoted themselves to protecting traditional values in the political realm: serving as the conscience of rulers—counseling them through moral suasions, remonstrating with them to rectify defective policies, chastising them for personal failings—sometimes at great personal risk. They offered a moral compass, based on learning and reflection, and acted as critics, moral educators, and disinterested proponents of the public good.[9]

THE FIFTH GREAT INVENTION

And how did one come to be a scholar-official? Through the *keju* system, which administered the imperial exam. While the Chinese were using examinations to select government officials in the Han dynasty (206 BC–AD 220) more than two thousand years ago, *keju* officially began in AD 605. It became the dominant way to select government officials in the Tang dynasty (AD 618–907), and it gained even more preeminence in the Song dynasty (AD 960–1279). *Keju* lasted for thirteen hundred years, until it was abolished in 1905 by the emperor of the Qing dynasty (AD 1644–1911). For good or for bad, *keju* was responsible for the continuity and antiquity of the Chinese civilization.

The format and content of the examinations varied slightly across dynasties, and there were interruptions at times of turmoil and during changes of dynasties. Still, the process and principles remained pretty much the same for the entire thirteen hundred years. The exams consistently probed knowledge of the Confucian classics, and their format was typically memorization and interpretation of the texts, as well as expository writing on current affairs and politics.

Examinations were typically offered at three levels: local, provincial, and national. They were norm referenced, meaning that only a certain number of examinees could succeed and be privileged to move to the next level. Success at each level earned the examinee a title and certain privileges, just as professional degrees do today. Depending on the time, those who succeeded at the most basic level could be excused from certain taxes and corvée (labor for the state) and would have the opportunity to be appointed a government official. The highest "degree" was *Jinshi*, awarded to winners of the national-level exam. A certain number of *Jinshi* were allowed to attend another final-level exam, held in the imperial court before the emperor. The winners were ranked based on their exam results, and the highest-ranked examinees climbed to the top of the bureaucracy.

Theoretically the examination was open to all male residents, regardless of family background, age, or years of studying, which meant that every individual had a shot at becoming a member of the ruling elite and thus acquiring wealth, social status, and power. This is why *keju* has been viewed as such an effective measure for social mobility in an otherwise hierarchical, dictatorial society. From the perspective of the rulers, *keju* was a tool to identify and recruit the most capable and virtuous individuals into government instead of relying on members of the hereditary noble class, which could become weak and corrupt as time went on.

In terms of its contribution to China and the world, the *keju* system is said to be the fifth great invention of China, along with gunpowder, the compass, paper, and movable type. As an essential element of the Chinese political system for more than a thousand years, the *keju* system had an impact on Chinese society and culture that cannot be overstated. Because of its apparent fairness, objectivity, and openness, *keju* gave birth to the idea of meritocracy, a core value in China and other Eastern Asian countries such as Korea, Japan, and Vietnam. These countries copied the *keju* system shortly after its invention in China. *Keju* also shaped East Asia's most fundamental, enduring educational values. So it is both ironic and understandable that Sun Yat-sen, the founding father of the Chinese republic, praised *keju* as the world's best education system and wanted to make sure that its tradition

In terms of its contribution to China and the world, the keju *system is said to be the fifth great invention of China, along with gunpowder, the compass, paper, and movable type.*

continued—even as he devoted his life to ending imperial rule.

In his proposed Five-Power Constitution, Sun added examination to the traditional legislative, judicial, and executive powers of government as a way to fix the problems of the American-style, three-power democracy. The American democracy, Sun observed, "often makes stupid mistakes," one of them the inability to elect the most competent leader. In 1921, Sun told the story of a doctor who lost an election to a rickshaw driver because the rickshaw driver was able to communicate with the voters, while the doctor was too knowledgeable to be understood. "Of the two candidates, the doctor certainly is more knowledgeable than the driver but he lost. This is the consequence of a system of popular election without examination."[10] Sun's Five-Power Constitution was successfully implemented by the Republic of China, which now includes executive, legislative, judicial, examination, and control branches of government (or yuan).

"Indeed, with the Chinese system of meritocracy in place, it is inconceivable that people as weak and incompetent as George W. Bush or Yoshihiko Noda of Japan could ever get to the top leadership position," wrote Zhang Weiwei, a professor at China's Fudan University, in a 2012 op-ed in the *New York Times*, affirming Sun's view almost a century later. Commenting on the coincidence of the US presidential election with the power transition that takes place in the Chinese Communist Party every ten years, Zhang noted that the Chinese meritocracy just might beat America's popular elections:

> Meritocratic governance is deeply-rooted in China's Confucian political tradition, which among other things allowed the country to develop and sustain for well over a millennium the *Keju* system, the world's first public exam process for selecting officials. China's political and institutional innovations so far have produced a system that has in many ways combined the best option of selecting well-tested leaders and the least bad option of ensuring the exit of bad leaders.[11]

THE IRONY OF GREAT INVENTIONS

Voltaire and his fellow Sinophiles would have been startled by the speed of Europe's shift from Sinophilia to Sinophobia. They'd be even more startled to find that their idolized polity not only wasn't emulated by European nations, but instead was shattered by European powers merely a century later. China's great inventions did not stop the Western assault; instead, the Western powers turned those inventions against China. They successfully weakened the Chinese Confucian tradition by spreading Christianity, using copies of the Bible printed, thanks to China, on paper with movable-type technology. They brought powerful warships all the way from Europe to China's doorstep, using the compass the Chinese invented. They delivered many humiliating defeats and garnered tremendous wealth from China using the great Chinese invention of gunpowder.

The fifth great invention, *keju*, did not help China either. The great Confucian tradition and the rational and intelligent scholar-officials failed to defend the great civilization against "the Western barbarians." In fact, the *keju* system has been held responsible for the decline of the Chinese empire.

When the European Jesuit missionaries sent home stories about the glorious Chinese emperor and inspired Sinomania in Europe, China had reached its peak in terms of economy and territory. For the previous millennium, China had been by far the most advanced and most prosperous country in the world. Its technological innovations far outpaced any other nation's until the Industrial Revolution. In the series Science and Civilisation in China, Cambridge University's Sinologist Joseph Needham and his collaborators have shown that China had many more than four great inventions. Since 1954, Cambridge University Press has published twenty-four books in this series.[12]

Yet all of these great inventions failed to turn China into a modern technological and scientific nation. Unlike modern technological advances, many of China's inventions were never improved to the level necessary to transform society. For example, the Chinese used their compass mainly to help find building locations and burial sites with good *fengshui*—not to navigate the oceans and expand across the globe as the West did. Gunpowder stopped at a level good enough for fireworks, but not for the modern weaponry that gave the West its military might.

Justin Yifu Lin, a former vice president of the World Bank and well-known professor of economics at Peking University, reviewed the literature about premodern China and concluded: "Most scholars believe that, as early as in the early period of Ming Dynasty (14th century), China had acquired all the major elements that were essential for the British industrial revolution in the 18th century." In other words, China was almost ready for the Industrial Revolution four hundred years before Great Britain was. "However, industrial revolution occurred in Britain instead of China and Chinese economy was quickly overtaken and lagged behind by western countries," writes Lin. "Why did the industrial revolution not originate from China, the place that first acquired all the major conditions?" Lin asks the question first posed by Max Weber, and Joseph Needham had puzzled over the same questions: "Why had China been so far in advance of other civilizations" and "Why is not China now ahead of the rest of world?"[13]

There's no doubt that *keju* was partly responsible for China's earlier great achievements. According to Lin, China was able to achieve so many technological and scientific innovations because of the size of its population. Rudimentary technological innovations can be made by accident. The probability of such accidents is the same for all societies, and thus the more people in a society, the higher the probability is of accidental inventions. "Before the industrial revolution in the 18th century, technological innovations were mainly realized through accidental discoveries in production process by craftsmen and peasants," writes Lin. "Because China had a large population, it had a large amount of craftsmen and peasants."[14]

People did, however, need a relatively stable society in order to engage in activities that might lead to discovery. They also needed time and certain resources. *Keju* helped build a unified nation with a large population, so it could have a large pool of accidental discoveries. *Keju* also provided relative stability and economic prosperity, so people could engage in productive activities pregnant with possibilities of accidental invention.

But *keju* was also the reason for China's failure to start the Industrial Revolution. After methodically refuting a number of existing hypotheses that attribute the lack of scientific revolution in China to economic reasons (land-people ratio or a repressive political environment), Lin found *keju*, the imperial exam system, to be the real reason:

> Because of this examination system, curious geniuses were diverted
> from learning mathematics and conducting controllable
> experiments. Because of this system, the geniuses could not

accumulate crucial human capital that was essential for the scientific revolution. As a result, the discoveries of natural phenomena could only be based on sporadic observations, and could not be upgraded into modern science, which was built upon mathematics and controlled experiments.[15]

A CLEVER PLOY OF SOCIAL CONTROL

The diversion of "curious geniuses" from mathematics and scientific experiment was a design feature of the imperial exam system. The entire population was diverted from pursuing anything that might challenge the Confucian orthodoxy and, hence, the imperial order. By design, the system rewarded obedience, encouraged compliance, and fostered homogeneous thinking.

As a system formally initiated by an emperor who seized the throne from his own boss, *keju* was first and foremost developed to prevent anyone else from repeating the emperor's coup. Yang Jian, Emperor Wen of the Sui dynasty (AD 581–618), served the Northern Zhou (AD 557–581) court as prime minister and a military general. Through bloody murders and military threat, Yang Jian forced the North Zhou emperor to abdicate the throne. Yang then accepted the position of emperor, "in response to people's wishes," in AD 581. Numerous victorious military campaigns later, he had unified China, joining a land that had been divided into warring kingdoms for more than three centuries.

As a system formally initiated by an emperor who seized the throne from his own boss, keju *was first and foremost developed to prevent anyone else from repeating the emperor's coup.*

The emperor's biggest concern was keeping China unified under his family's rule. Learning from his own example, he realized he needed a way to weaken the hereditary power of certain families and tribes. Thus, he needed to find people who could help govern the country without relying on the existing ruling class. He also needed a way to prevent capable talents from rising against the empire and to reinforce among his subjects the need to obey the rightful rule of the Son of Heaven.

We can't know how much Emperor Wen planned and strategized, but the establishment of *keju* accomplished every one of his goals. Prior to the Sui dynasty, China's rulers had relied on recommendation and inspection to appoint government officials. In the Han dynasty (206 BC–AD 220), most positions of the bureaucracy were filled with individuals recommended by prominent aristocrats and local officials. Emperor Wu of the Han dynasty did implement a partial exam system in which the candidates for the exam were based on recommendations from local officials but the final selection was based on the results of the exam. However, connections and recommendations from the existing elites weighed much more heavily than the exam results. The next dynasties implemented the nine rank system, in which imperial officials were put in place to assess candidates nominated by local officials. Family lines were explicitly used as a criterion for selection, and connections to existing officials were crucial.

To minimize the influence of hereditary power, Emperor Wen improved on the practices of Emperor Wu. First, the recommendation prerequisite was removed so everyone was eligible to take the exam. Second, selection was based strictly on performance in the exam. To make the process even more resistant to corruption and the influence of the powerful, future emperors began to hide the names of the candidates from the examiners. These changes not only reduced the influence of hereditary power but also enlarged the candidate pool, making it easier for the emperors to find the most talented people.

More important, *keju* presented itself as an objective, transparent, and universally accessible system for social mobility. It gave hope to the masses. Regardless of a man's family lineage and economic conditions, he could achieve power, wealth, and social status as long as he worked hard and succeeded at the exams. In imperial China, government positions were held in the highest esteem. They stood at the top of the professional hierarchy, which ranked craftsmen and merchants at the bottom. Even the richest merchants wanted their sons to gain recognition and raise the family profile through the imperial exam. *Keju* became the most attractive option for anyone with the slightest ambition—and it left no incentive to pursue anything else.

The *keju* exams were intensely competitive, and the success rate was quite low. It could take years of hard work to pass even the first level, and many never did. Still, the rewards were so attractive that the arduous journey rarely deterred anyone from trying. "For ten years no one cares about you when you are studying in a cold room," the Chinese tell their young people, "but

> *"For ten years no one cares about you when you are studying in a cold room, but the entire world will know you as soon as you succeed."*

the entire world will know you as soon as you succeed." That saying, which sums up the hardship and reward of education, originated in the *keju* era.

The irresistible appeal of *keju* gave the emperor a powerful and cost-effective tool of social control. Through the exams, he could steer people's thinking because they all devoted their resources to studying his required material: the Confucian texts, which advocate obedience and respect for order and harmony.

For thirteen hundred years, Chinese emperors were delivered a homogeneous and obedient citizenry in three ways. First, through the exams, they recruited individuals who demonstrated the greatest commitment to Confucian thinking to help defend the status quo and perpetuate the regime. These fortunate scholar-officials became not only devout defenders but also capable promoters of imperial rule. Skilled writers and speakers of Confucian thinking, they were living examples of the benefits of studying for the exam. Second, even those who failed at the exams became defenders and promoters, because often they were hired as teachers to help prepare future generations for the exams. Third, after decades of studying the Confucian texts, even if a man did not become a believer, he would have little time, energy, and resources left to develop the skills, knowledge, and independent ideas needed for a rebellion.

The outcomes of *keju* were exactly what the emperors wished. "All heroes under the sun have fallen into my trap," Emperor Taizong exclaimed with gleeful pride as he watched new successful candidates of *keju* file into his court. Taizong, was the grandson of Emperor Wen. He had encouraged his father to rise against Sui and helped him established the Tang dynasty in AD 618. Taizong became the second emperor of Tang after killing his brother, the crown prince designated to succeed his father as emperor. He then further improved *keju* and made it a regular and permanent practice in his court. In the Sui dynasty's thirty-eight years of rule, *keju* was offered only four or five times and selected only twelve candidates in total. But Taizong offered *keju* annually, and he also presided over special exams to recruit other talents. However, these special exams, which could have given China a more diverse set of talents, were not continued after his rule. He has been credited with codifying *keju* for future emperors as a powerful method of recruiting talent and cultivating obedience. "Emperor Taizong had truly a long-term strategy, for it gave white hair to all heroes," wrote the Tang dynasty poet Zhao Gu.

The obedience *keju* fostered was so attractive that even the non-Han emperors adopted the system after taking over the reign of China. The Mongols, for example, who defeated the Song dynasty in the thirteenth century, eventually adopted *keju*. The Manchu rulers, after conquering China and establishing the Qing dynasty in the mid-seventeenth century, continued *keju* and made it the only way for the Han people to gain social mobility.

CHANGE WITHOUT DIFFERENCE

Thanks to *keju*, Taizong and his successors enjoyed generations of citizens who were obedient, compliant, and skilled at literary work. They had similar thoughts, similar skills, and similar talents. As historians John King Fairbank and Merle Goldman observed in their book *China: A New History*:

> Under the empire, men of letters had come to be almost universally
> examination candidates and therefore classicists and conservatives.
> Most of the great achievements of Chinese literature had come
> within this framework of acceptance of the social order and central
> authority. No monastic sanctuaries, no clash of sectarian faiths, no
> division between church and state were allowed, as in Europe, to
> spawn diversity.[16]

These men were excellent guardians of the existing order, and they helped maintain a unified nation. Their minds were steeped in Confucian philosophy, which forbade them to have any unorthodox thoughts. Their lack of knowledge and skills outside the narrowly defined domains of the imperial exam rendered them incapable of putting up a rebellion, even if the thought had occurred to them. "It takes forever for *xiucai* to launch a successful revolution" is a popular Chinese saying that captures the inadequacies of traditional intellectuals. *Xiucai* was one of the titles granted to successful candidates of the imperial exam, and it became a generic reference to educated people in China. This is why, in two thousand years, virtually none of the hundreds of regime changes was started or finished by scholar-officials or anyone else with the highest level of Chinese education.

The scholar-officials had finely trained memories, but they were not independent or critical thinkers, nor were they knowledgeable beyond the Confucian classics and certain forms of literary writing. Although they were excellent at perpetuating the past, they failed at inventing the future. In fact, they were a powerful force resisting the invention of a new future. This conservatism was fine for a closed society with an agrarian economy. In that system, peace, stability, and benevolent rulers were far more productive than revolutionary ideas and different perspectives. If the world had stopped in the seventeenth century, China would still be the most prosperous society and *keju* the most effective way to create and maintain such a society, just as those Jesuit missionaries and European philosophers had imagined.

But the Industrial Revolution changed everything, ushering in a new era in which change became the constant, innovation the norm, and diversity of talents the source of social development. In this new era, *keju*, which reinforced conservative thinking and homogeneity, changed from a blessing to a curse.

In this new era, keju, which reinforced conservative thinking and homogeneity, changed from a blessing to a curse.

The year 1840 marked the beginning of China's modern history of defeat, frustration, and humiliation. That's when the British government sent in forces, armed with far superior military technology, to force China to take in more opium and other Western goods. The Chinese launched a futile and costly resistance, but their spears and traditional firearms were no match for the modern muskets and cannons, nor were their junks for the steam-powered warships. In 1842, after two years of military defeats, representatives of the Chinese emperor began negotiations with representatives of Queen Victoria. They climbed aboard the *HMS Cornwallis*, anchored on the Yangtze River at Nanjing, with British warships poised to attack the city. The resulting Treaty of Nanjing forced China to open five ports for trade, pay $21 million in reparations to Britain over three years, and cede Hong Kong to the British queen. Even worse, the treaty imposed a fixed tariff rate, essentially allowing a foreign country to set the rate in China; gave British subjects extraterritorial privileges at treaty ports; and granted most-favored-nation status to Britain. The Treaty of Nanjing set a precedent for China's foreign relations with other countries, and its effects lasted for almost a century.

Although the Treaty of Nanjing brought the First Opium War to an end, it did not end the export of opium to China or war against China. Quite the contrary. The amount of opium coming into China jumped from thirty thousand chests in the 1830s to seventy thousand chests in 1858—twenty years after the treaty—when the Second Opium War broke out. This time, the French joined the British. The Anglo-French army pushed all the way to Beijing, forced the entire imperial court to flee, and robbed and burned the old Summer Palace. The war ended with the Chinese empire opening more ports to foreign trade, ceding the territories of Kowloon, permitting foreign legations in Beijing, allowing Christian missionary activities, legalizing opium imports, and agreeing to pay 2 million taels of silver in indemnity to Britain and France. (The tael was a commonly used weight and currency measure in China at the time.)

More defeats and treaties would come. By the time the Qing dynasty collapsed in 1911, China had signed hundreds of "unequal treaties," always in the wake of military defeat or threat, with virtually all Western powers and Japan. It had ceded vast amounts of land to Russia, Japan, Britain, and other countries; opened almost all major cities as treaty ports; paid hundreds of millions of dollars in reparations; and compromised both its sovereignty and its dignity.

What the First Opium War did end, though, was the idea that China was the world, or at least the most privileged and civilized center of the universe—a view that had been reinforced by emperors and their scholar-officials for thousands of years. The admission in the Treaty of Nanjing that Britain was equal to China was a historical transformation. A mere fifty years before, in 1793, when Lord George Macartney went to Beijing as the first British ambassador, he refused to kowtow to Emperor Qianlong despite the insistence of his host. Macartney was considered a bearer of tribute from Britain rather than a guest. One of his missions was to convey Britain's desire to establish trade with China. But the emperor rejected the suggestion, declaring in a letter to King George III: "Our dynasty's majestic virtue has penetrated unto every country under Heaven, and Kings of all nations have offered their costly tribute by land and sea. As your Ambassador can see for himself, we possess all things. I set no value on objects strange or ingenious, and have no use for your country's manufactures."[17]

The Opium War taught the Chinese that the West had something they could use: modern technology. But they still maintained the belief that the Chinese way was superior. As a result, the progressive scholars and government officials began the self-strengthening movement, also known as the Westernization movement. "Chinese learning as the base, Western learning as utility," they insisted. The idea was to maintain Chinese culture as the core values and adopt Western technology for its utilitarian value only: Westernization the Chinese way.

The movement's most important goal was to improve military technology, which was perhaps the only thing deemed worth learning from the West anyway. The emperor established Western-style shipyards and arsenals and brought in Westerners to teach the Chinese how to manufacture warships, guns, and cannons on the assumption that the superior Chinese wisdom and intelligence, plus the technology they would learn from Western countries, would enable the Chinese to defeat the Westerners with their own technology. But the rifles and ships built in China were more expensive and of lower quality than the ones directly imported from the West. So the Chinese also purchased guns, cannons, and warships. Equipped with a modern fleet purchased from Britain and Germany, China established a powerful modern navy that in 1888 was number one in Asia. This peerless navy was promptly crushed in 1894—not by a Western country this time but by Japan. China was forced to sign yet one more "unequal treaty" that paid Japan 200 million taels of silver in indemnity, ceded the Liaodong Peninsula and Taiwan with its nearby islands to Japan, and opened more treaty ports.

Defeat by Japan made the Chinese realize that superior technology did not guarantee victory and their problem went much deeper than guns and warships. *Keju*, the imperial examination and system, was the root cause of China's defeat. "The cession of Taiwan and Liaodong was not caused by the imperial court, but by *bagu*; the two-million taels indemnity should be blamed on the imperial court, but *bagu*," a reform-minded scholar, Kang Youwei, told Emperor Guangxu in 1898.[18] *Bagu* or *Baguwen* (eight-part essay) was the dominant format of *keju* during the Qing dynasty. *Bagu* asked the test takers to interpret original sentences from one of the Confucian classics. The interpretation must be either three hundred or five hundred Chinese characters long and contain eight predefined parts.

"Today's sufferings are the consequence of uneducated people in China, which resulted from selecting officials through *bagu*," Kang informed the emperor. "Those who study for *bagu* don't read books written after the Qin and Han Dynasties, let alone attempt to understand happenings in other countries around the world, but they could achieve high positions in the government. Thus despite the large number of officials, we cannot find anyone to be capable of carrying out important tasks." "You are right," Emperor Guangxu agreed. "Westerners pursue useful knowledge, but all we Chinese pursue are useless knowledge."[19]

At the suggestion of Kang Youwei and other like-minded intellectuals, Emperor Guangxu launched a battery of reform efforts: abolishing *keju*, establishing Western-style universities, translating Western books into Chinese, and sending students to Japan and Western countries. The reform, however, lasted only 103 days. It ended in a bloody crackdown by Empress Dowager Cixi, Emperor Guangxu's aunt, who had installed him as the emperor at the age of four. Guangxu was put under house arrest, Kang Youwei fled to Japan, and six prominent reform leaders were executed in public.

Keju survived, but not for long. Another military defeat three years later made even Empress Dowager Cixi a reformer. In 1900, military forces of the alliance of eight nations (Austria-Hungary, France, Germany, Italy, Japan, Russia, the Untied Kingdom, and the United States) marched into Beijing to rescue the diplomatic legations under siege by the Boxer rebels. Cixi and her court officials fled to Xi'an. After yet one more "unequal treaty" (the Boxer Protocol) that cost China 450 million taels of silver as indemnity to the eight nations, Empress Dowager Cixi launched a set of moderate reforms and stopped using *Baguwen* as a form of *keju*.

Her actions did not calm the rising anger toward the imperial court and the people's frustration with the exam. On September 2, 1905, a group of powerful military leaders, governors, and high-level officials—including Yuan Shikai, the second president of the Republic of China, who invited Frank Goodnow to consult on the Chinese constitution—sent a plea to the imperial court. To save China, "we must start to popularize schools; to popularize schools, we must start by ending *keju*," reasoned Yuan Shikai and his cosigners. Confronted by such a powerful group, the imperial court did not feel it had a choice. On the same day, Emperor Guangxu sent out a decree to the entire empire: "All *keju* exams are to end."[20] Six years later, in 1911, the Qing dynasty was replaced by the Republic of China, ending over two thousand years of imperial rule.

For two thousand years, China had remained the same, despite the many changes in dynasties and emperors. The changes brought in new emperors but no new ideas. The new emperors simply repeated what their predecessors did. There were good and bad emperors, periods of war and periods of peace, times of unification and times of division, but the essential social structure, governing principles of human relationships, views of human nature and the natural environment, and moral and ethical code remained the same. There was no Renaissance, no Enlightenment, no Industrial Revolution.

Before the Western powers arrived, the Chinese wanted to keep their way forever because they were sure it was the best way. The humiliation that the West delivered made the Chinese reconsider their position, and ultimately they decided that the Chinese way must be abandoned. It was holding China back from modernization. Borrowing technology was not sufficient to develop a modern nation; China needed people with different capabilities and thinking from what the emperors desired. China ended its imperial rule and exam.

What China decided to abandon a century ago is now being highly praised— and copied by the West—in the most recent wave of Sinomania. What have been identified as the great attributes of the Chinese culture, society, and education that

Has the world changed so much that what did not work before works now?

led to China's recent rise as a world power are the very attributes the Enlightenment Sinophiles praised three hundred years ago—suggesting that China, despite its efforts to change, remains the same today as it was three hundred years ago, or two thousand years ago. Yet these traits have been generally agreed on as the cause of China's last decline. Has the world changed so much that what did not work before works now? Or is the recent rise of China also the result of what made ancient China prosperous—and like China's ancient prosperity, will it soon end, unless transformative changes occur?

3

GOVERNANCE WITHOUT GOVERNING
The Retreat of Authoritarianism and China's Economic Boom

The first action that altered China's modern history was not the result of careful planning by the elite leaders of the Communist government in Beijing, but a secret meeting of eighteen peasants in a remote village. The peasants were not motivated by grand aspirations to change history or restore China's greatness. They acted on instinct, driven by the simple need to avoid fleeing from their homes or starving to death.

The historic meeting took place on November 24, 1978, about two years after the passing of Chairman Mao, who led the Chinese Communist Party to defeat the Nationalists. Mao founded the People's Republic of China in 1949. His government spent the next thirty years engaged in Soviet-style political campaigns and illusionary economic activities, all designed to build China into a Communist superstate that could rival the Western imperialists. After three decades of collectivization movements, China practically eradicated private property ownership, wiped out commercial activities, suppressed all capitalist thoughts, and turned all citizens into members of the state. All economic activities were planned and dictated by the state.

The vast peasant population in China was, just like the city dwellers, confined to the place where they were born by the *hukou* system, a population management mechanism to limit mobility and thus potential unrest. Used by various Chinese emperors, *hukou* essentially "made the state a feudal master over its farmers," notes Ted Fishman in *China Inc.: How the Rise of the Next Superpower Challenges America and the World.* "By 1960, the Communists had all but sealed most of the country's people off, not just from the world, but from China's own cities."[1]

As members of the state workforce, the peasants worked in commune teams and followed farming programs rigidly pre-scribed and seriously enforced by the government. They had to grow exactly what the government told them and in ways the government dictated, regardless of their local context. "All farmers in China know this joke," write Guidi Chen and Chuntao Wu, well known for their writings about Chinese agriculture. "There are only four people in China who know about farming—Secretaries of the Community Party Commission of the province, the prefec-ture, the county, and commune. They tell the farmers what to grow, when to sow, how much to grow, when to harvest and how much they will receive at the end of the year."[2]

The results of these tight controls were disastrous. "In the 20 years between 1958 and 1978, Chinese society was practically in a state of stagnation," summarized Deng Xiaoping, the reform-minded leader who has been credited for the reforms responsible for China's recent surge. "Neither the national economy nor people's living standards had significant improvement."[3]

In 1978, China was one of the world's poorest nations, with nearly one-third of a population over 900 million living under the poverty line set by China. Using the international standard of poverty (per capita cost of living below $1.00 a day), more than half of China's population lived in poverty.[4] Its per capita GDP in 1980 was $193, lower than Chad's and Burkina Faso's. The annual income for Chinese farmers was 133 renminbi (RMB)—about $19.00—in 1978.

Then came the "secret meeting" of eighteen peasants in an isolated village in Anhui Province, a meeting that would soon be enshrined as the beginning of the new China.

THE PEASANTS WHO SAVED CHINA

"It was just after dinner on November 24, 1978," Chen and Wu write in *Stories of Xiaogang Village*, recounting the meeting that changed China:

> *Xiaogang* Village, without electricity, let alone street lights, was
> already in pitch darkness. The cities might still be busy and noisy,
> but there was only complete silence in the village, for most of the
> village members had gone to bed.

> All of a sudden, the dogs began barking. Eighteen men of the
> Xiaogang production team sneaked out of their houses. They
> quietly walked toward the house of Yan Lihua in the piercingly cold
> northwestern wind, heads down and arms wrapped around them.[5]

The meeting site had been chosen after much deliberation, according to Chen and Wu. Yan Lihua lived alone in a five-room house at the west end of the village, away from others and thus ideal for keeping the meeting a secret. His grandfather, parents, and two brothers had all starved to death during the 1961 famine.

The meeting had to be secret because at the time, such meetings were illegal. What the villagers decided to do that night could have landed them in prison, even sentenced them to death. Their decision was to divvy up the village land and assign plots to each family, allowing them to work their own land. "I have two conditions," Yan Hongchang, the village leader, reportedly said. "First, Xiaogang Village has been receiving grains from the government every year, but from next year on, we must set aside enough grains for the government and collective upon our first harvest." Yan's second condition was to keep this a secret: "What we will do is to maintain the appearance of working in teams. We will keep it from the above. No one is allowed to tell outsiders or our government leaders. If you do, you are the enemy to all of us." He promised his fellow villagers, "If you agree to these two conditions, I dare to take the lead." Their response was even bolder than what he'd asked: "If our team leader is imprisoned for breaking up the team," one of the villagers said, "the rest of the villagers will take care of his land and support his children until [they reach the age of] eighteen." The eighteen peasants drew up a simple agreement in plain language: "We divvy up the land and assign to each family. Head of each family sign and stamp to agree that if it works, we guarantee payment to the government and will not ask the government for food anymore. If not, we leaders will rest in peace even if imprisoned or beheaded. All members of the team also promise to support our children until they are eighteen years old." Below the agreement were twenty names, each representing one family in the village. The peasants signed the document with red fingerprints. Two families were absent because the heads of their households had not returned from a begging trip. Their relatives signed the document on their behalf.

Team leader Yan Hongchang then dated the agreement: December 1978. This was a calculation error. The villagers were used to the Chinese lunar calendar, but Yan wanted to make it as official and formal as possible, so he decided to use the Gregorian calendar. Normally there is a one to two months' difference between the two calendars. Since it was October on the lunar calendar, Yan thought it must be December. He realized his mistake only two days later when he looked at a calendar on display at the state-owned Supply and Consumption Society on a shopping trip.

The mistake hardly mattered. In the next year, this village of twenty families produced sixty thousand kilograms of grains, about the total amount produced by the village between 1955 and 1970: their gamble had paid off. The secret was quickly discovered by neighboring villages—and, of course, the government.

Fortunately, the top leaders were ready for change, and this risky experiment became a model for reform in China. By 1982, China had dismantled most communes and adopted what the government called the family responsibility system, which in essence restored family farming and gave each family independent control over its livelihood. As a result, crop yields rose, and the national grain harvest shot up from 304.8 million tons in 1978 to 407.3 million tons in 1984, basically solving the food shortages that had plagued China for the previous three decades.

In the next year, these twenty families produced sixty thousand kilograms of grains, about the total amount produced by the village between 1955 and 1970. Their gamble had paid off.

The December 1978 agreement has been on exhibit in the Museum of Chinese Revolution, in Tiananmen Square in Beijing, as a significant artifact of China's modern development. The story of the meeting has been told and retold by state media as the beginning of China's success for more than three decades. As appealing as this Hollywood "little-guy-saves-the-world" story is, it's hard to believe eighteen peasants had the capacity or power to change China. But they happened to do the right thing at the right time under the right leader. Had they done the same five years earlier, their fears would have been realized: they would have been punished like so many others who had dared to challenge the communist government.

But the Chinese government was ready to change. A month later, in December 1978, the Chinese Communist Party held its own historic meeting, and not in secret. The Third Plenum of the

Central Committee of the Chinese Communist Party was held in Beijing from December 18 to December 22. The four-day meeting ended Mao's dogmatic ideology and began a new era of reform and openness led by Deng Xiaoping. The peasants of Xiaogang Village became an excellent example of the new China, and they have been not only pardoned but also lauded as heroes.

China clearly does not owe its recent rise to a benevolent and foresighted leader or to its well-educated scholar-officials, but to a group of uneducated peasants desperate to make a living. The moral of the story is not that commoners can challenge authority, but that when commoners are left alone, they can do great things. The story illustrates the constraining effect of government planning and the liberating power of autonomy. When autonomy is granted, people become more motivated and, because they are free to act, more creative in designing solutions to their problems.

THE FIRST ENTREPRENEURS

China's recent economic growth is not the result of wise planning. It is the result of government retreating from overregulation. Since 1978, the Communist government has dramatically loosened its control of economic and social activities, making room for individuals to exercise their own free will. One of the most significant changes has been the legalization of private enterprises.

About the same time that the peasants in Xiaogang Village held their secret meeting, an illiterate, self-labeled "fool" merchant in the same Anhui Province challenged China's leaders again. Nian Guangjiu, founder of the Fool's Sunflower Seeds, a household brand name in China, employed twelve people to help with his sunflower seed business. According to the Marxist doctrine about exploitation, a private business with over eight employees becomes capitalist and thus engages in exploitation. Was Nian a capitalist and therefore should have been banished from Communist China? The debate raged not only among academics but also among political leaders. It lasted until 1982 when China's leader, Deng Xiaoping, settled the debate with a typical Deng-style verdict: Let's wait and see. By then, Nian had expanded his business to over 140 employees. Deng's verdict saved him and hundreds of thousands of other merchants.[6]

"Wait and see" was a clever political strategy employed by Deng Xiaoping to maneuver through a tough political situation. Privatization and marketization were still considered a threat to dogmatic communism. Instead of fighting head-on, the pragmatic Deng famously used his "cat theory" to put the issue to rest: "It does not matter if a cat is black or white. It is a good cat as long as it catches mice." Instead of arguing over communism versus capitalism, he directed the nation's attention to economic development. What did it matter if progress was communist or capitalist as long as it improved people's lives and strengthened the nation? "Cross the river by feeling the stones" was another Deng maxim that made room for the Chinese to explore different (often illegal at the time) forms of economic activity.

Alas, Nian got in trouble again. In 1987, he was charged with embezzlement. He protested the charge and was rumored to have slapped the Communist Party leader of the local government. How could it be "embezzlement" if he spent his own money? The embezzlement charge was dropped, but Nian was still given a three-year prison sentence in 1991 for hooliganism. Once again, Deng saved him. On his famous Tour of the South in 1992 to restart China's economic reform, which had stalled after the massive student demonstration in 1989, Deng, now retired from his official position but still the most powerful political leader in China, told Nian's story: "At the beginning of reform in the countryside, there was the incident of the Fool's Sunflower Seeds. Many people were uncomfortable with him because he became a millionaire. They wanted to do something about it, but I said no, because if we touched him, people would doubt our policy. The loss outweighed the gain."[7]

Nian was released almost immediately. This was his third time in jail. In 1963, he'd been jailed for peddling fish and in 1966, for peddling nuts. Reflecting on his prison terms, Nian was extremely grateful to Deng Xiaoping: "I know he did not only speak out for me. He spoke out for many fools."[8]

These "many fools" were China's first entrepreneurs. Despite the severe consequences of engaging in private commercial activities in a culture that looked down on merchants, a large number of individuals secretly took on entrepreneurial activities prior to 1978. They knew that if the government discovered their activities, they would be jailed or even put to death. But like Nian and the peasants in Xiaogang, their need to survive was so strong that they took the risk. With nearly 1 billion people living in impoverished conditions, there were plenty of people desperate to make a decent living at any cost. All they needed was Deng Xiaoping to speak out for them.

LET IT BE (OR GOVERNANCE WITHOUT INTERFERENCE)

Deng Xiaoping spoke out not only for Nian and his fellow peddlers and for the peasants who divvied up the state land, but also for all aspiring entrepreneurs in China. Although he never held the official highest position, Deng became China's de facto leader in 1978. Under his leadership, the Chinese government went through historic reforms to allow its citizens to make their own decisions.

First, in 1978, the Third Plenum of the Central Committee of the Chinese Communist Party gave peasants permission to make decisions about their farming activities and to trade the surplus of their production. More important, it allowed farmers to move away from their land to work in the mushrooming "township and

village enterprises"—small-scale industrial or commercial businesses owned by local villages or township—work for other
farmers, or set up shops in the city to sell agricultural produce.

The 800 million peasants thoroughly enjoyed their new autonomy. It was they who supplied the first fuel for China's global
ascent.[9] They became much more productive as farmers, so they
had surpluses. They began to sell their surpluses to each other
and to city dwellers. Some farmers seized the opportunity to
become full-time merchants, entrepreneurs who collected surplus
agricultural goods from individual farmers and sold them in the
city. Others specialized in transporting these goods over long dis-
tances, making a profit from price differences. Still others began
to focus on vegetables, meat, poultry, and fish instead of the traditional rice, wheat, and corn in response to the needs of their new
customers. That shift brought them enough capital to develop
their small businesses into large enterprises. They began to employ
their fellow villagers, which provided more opportunities for
others to earn cash and improve their standard of living.

Over the past thirty years, according to the World Bank, China
has lifted more than 600 million people out of poverty. The proportion of Chinese people living under the poverty line dropped
from 85 percent in 1981 to 15.9 percent in 2005, and most of that
decrease had been achieved in the first decade after 1978.[10]

Farmers also began to venture into entirely new markets,
making and selling daily necessities such as clothing, shoes, and
household supplies. The Communist government had either
completely neglected or deliberately ignored daily consumer
products. Moreover, to curtail capitalism, it had also instituted an
extremely inflexible distribution system. As a result, even the most
basic necessities, such as salt, oil, food, clothing, and paper, were
in short supply and had to be rationed. The empty shelves and
cold attendants in state-run stores spelled opportunity for the
newly liberated farmers, especially those in areas where land was
limited. Wenzhou, a mountainous area in southeastern Zhejiang

Province where there was little land suitable for farming—on average, half of 0.08 acre—became the first hotbed of private enterprise. Wenzhou merchants became famous all over China as they moved about the country selling their wares and buying raw materials. Like Xiaogang Village, Wenzhou also became a model and experiment field for the new economy. As a result, it quickly became one of the wealthiest areas in China. Gross domestic product in Wenzhou had jumped from 1.32 billion RMB in 1978 to 258.8 billion RMB in 2009, almost a two-hundred-fold increase.

In 1979, in addition to granting farmers economic freedom, the government allowed city dwellers the freedom to operate small businesses. Faced with 8 million unemployed youth, most of them who had just returned from their "reeducation" in remote rural areas, and other ex-convicts, the Chinese government permitted the establishment of individually operated repair shops, artisan crafts, retail stands, restaurants, and other service businesses. These individually owned businesses are called *getihu*. In 1980, a nineteen-year-old girl in Wenzhou was granted the first *getihu* license. By 1999, the number of *getihu* in China had grown to over 30 million. By 2013, it had surpassed 40 million, with some 80 million people working as or for *getihu*.[11] Many of the *getihu* evolved into private enterprises as they gained more capital and expanded their businesses.

Economic freedom paid off for China. It improved productivity in the countryside and solved employment problems in the city. It generated capital for investment and a large consumer base able and eager to buy goods and services. Furthermore, the early entrepreneurs served as examples, motivating many others to be more enterprising. With their newly acquired wealth, the pioneer entrepreneurs also forced the Chinese to reexamine some of their cultural values. Seeing uneducated peasants and ex-convicts becoming millionaires made the traditional elites—city dwellers and government employees, that is, almost all of whom had secure public sector jobs at the time—begin to question their own choices. As a result, some began to abandon their "iron rice bowl" (secure job) and *xiahai*—"enter the sea"—which means to join or start a private business.

Among the many who "entered the sea," Liu Chuanzhi is perhaps the best known. He quit his position at the Chinese Academy of Sciences in 1984 and started a computer company that eventually became Lenovo, one of the largest computer makers in the world. It purchased IBM's microcomputer business some twenty years later.

Increased productivity on Chinese farms also resulted in a massive number of eager and hungry laborers who would work for any price under any conditions. They were obedient and compliant: the Confucian values that had been inculcated in every generation for thousands of years had been reinforced by thirty years of Communist government.

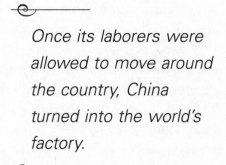

Once its laborers were allowed to move around the country, China turned into the world's factory.

These hard-working and tractable farmers proved an irresistible workforce for global manufacturers looking for cheap and easy-to-manage laborers. Companies could keep their labor and management costs as low as possible because this docile workforce could be organized and mobilized to fit their changing needs. Once its laborers were allowed to move around the country, China turned into the world's factory. By 2012, one of every three Chinese citizens of work age (fifteen to sixty-four) was a migrant worker, giving China a total of more than 260 million migrant workers.[12]

In addition, the booming private sector pushed the Chinese government to reform its state-owned enterprises. According to Justin Yifu Lin, a Chinese economist and former vice president of the World Bank, China's private enterprises became more productive than state-owned enterprises.[13] Because they did not have the same access to resources and markets as the government-owned enterprises, they had to act more creatively and competitively. As a result, they worked harder; had better management, better services, and better products; and could be more flexible and responsive to markets. To save the state-owned enterprises, the government had to learn from the private enterprises. The lesson? To grant the state-owned enterprises more autonomy.

When he spoke out for the peasants of Xiaogang and Nian Guangjiu (the sunflower seeds peddler), Deng Xiaoping didn't have a road map to China's ultimate economic prosperity. "This was not something I figured out...This was a surprise," he told a Yugoslavia delegation in 1987, referring to the rapid economic development in China's rural areas. "Our rural reforms have been developing rather fast and farmers have become very motivated. The development of the village and township industries took us by complete surprise...but these are not the achievement of the central government...If the central government has anything to do with this [achievement], that is we made the right policy to give them the autonomy."[14]

Although Deng was talking about the achievement in rural areas, his words are true for China's economic development over the past three decades. It was not foresight or wise planning by the central government that led to China's global rise. On the contrary, it was gradual withdrawal of government planning and regulation to create an environment that allowed people to exercise their autonomy. As Deng said, if the government deserved any credit, it was for leaving people alone and letting them be— which had been the fundamental principle of good governance in ancient times.

Like Bruce Lee's art of fighting without fighting, governance without governing was the highest form of government in traditional Chinese philosophy. Rooted in the Taoist thinking of no interference and following nature, Confucius was the first to utter the words "*wu wei er zhi*" (governing without action) and connect the phrase to government: "May not Shun [one of the most respected leaders of ancient China and thus a model for all rulers] be instanced as having governed efficiently without exertion? What did he do? He did nothing but gravely and reverently occupy his royal seat."[15] In Chinese history, when emperors followed this philosophy, they often achieved great prosperity. The two most prosperous periods in Chinese history, set forth as examples for emperors, are the early Han dynasty under Emperors Wen and Jing and early Tang dynasty under Emperor Taizong, the one who popularized *keju*.

THE COKE BATTLE

The Chinese government not only freed its people to work, but also allowed them the autonomy to consume. "Under the policies of Deng Xiaoping's 'market socialism,'" wrote Russell Belk and Nan Zhou, researchers at the University of Utah, in 1987, "consumers are being allowed as well as encouraged to want things that would have been totally unthinkable at the time of Mao Zedong's death a decade ago."[16] With nearly 1 billion people suddenly allowed to consume more than necessities, China became an irresistible market for any manufacturer.

Coca-Cola was one of the first to reenter that market after being banished from the Middle Kingdom for thirty years. Coke's success was great for the company, but even greater for the world's relationship with China. If the Opium Wars had the effect of making the Chinese realize the superiority of Western technology, the battle to reintroduce Coke had the effect of addicting the Chinese to Western consumer goods. The many twists and turns of Coke's reentry also forced changes in government regulations, created new business models for China, and pioneered direct foreign investment. Most important, it won an ideological battle by convincing the Communist leaders that consuming Western goods was neither capitalist nor an act of treason.

China's recent growth has been the result of a series of policies that have been generally lumped together as reform and opening up. If the stories of the peasants in Xiaogang Village and the Fool's Sunflower Seeds exemplify the domestic reforms, the return of Coca-Cola illustrates China opening up to the outside world.

Coca-Cola had nurtured dreams of returning to China ever since 1949, when it was ousted as the Communists took control of the country. In 1972, it set up an office in Beijing, shortly after the PRC replaced Taiwan as the sovereign country in the United Nations. In 1976, it approached the Chinese Liaison Office in the United States to express its intention to export products and establish bottling plants in China. Tong Zhiguang, then secretary of commerce in the Liaison Office and later vice minister of the Chinese Ministry of Foreign Trade, met with the Coca-Cola team but told them that China was not ready. He later explained why to the author of *Thirty Years of Battle: Personal Experiences with the Four Great Debates of Reform and Opening-up*: "Chinese born after the founding of New China have only seen Coca-Cola in movies, and the Coca-Cola in movies have always been associated with American soldiers. After the Korean War, Coca-Cola meant far more than a drink. China could not accept Coca-Cola because it represented the Western lifestyle."[17]

Coca-Cola's prospects began to look better after the death of Mao in 1976. A year later, Tong returned to China to work for the state-owned China National Cereals, Oils, and Foodstuffs Import and Export (COFCO), the government's exclusive importer and exporter for the entire food industry. A Coca-Cola executive invited Tong to another meeting in Beijing and told him that their primary target consumers in China were not the Chinese but foreign tourists. Furthermore, the company had no relationship with American soldiers, the executive said. It was only a business that made money by selling sweetened carbonated water. Put simply, Coca-Cola wanted to be wherever there was a desire for its product.[18]

Tong seemed to have been convinced. He brought the issue to his company, which then sought permission from the central government to start talks with Coca-Cola. In 1978, COFCO, holding a hand-written permission slip from Vice Premier Li Xiannian, who later became China's president, began substantive negotiations with Coca-Cola at the Beijing Hotel, where another meeting, at a much higher level, was taking place on the same floor at the same time. President Jimmy Carter's diplomats were talking with the Chinese about normalizing the US-China relationship. On December 13, 1978, Coca-Cola and COFCO signed their agreement: Coca-Cola would set up bottling plants and sell its products in major Chinese cities and tourist areas. Until the plants were built, Coca-Cola would ship products to China. Days later, the US and Chinese governments released a joint communiqué to normalize their diplomatic relations.

The first three thousand bottles of Coke arrived in Beijing from Hong Kong in 1979. Foreign media gave the auspicious event almost hour-by-hour coverage. Coca-Cola had become the first foreign company to sell in Communist China.

But the construction of the first bottling plant didn't go as smoothly as the first shipment. Even selecting a location proved a challenge. Coca-Cola initially wanted to build in Shanghai, where it had its first plant in 1927. But Shanghai rejected the offer vehemently, condemning the acceptance of Coca-Cola as a national betrayal by which China would enslave itself to foreigners, import the American lifestyle, and damage national industries. The first plant ended up in a Beijing factory that prepared Peking duck. And with that compromise, Coca-Cola became the first foreign enterprise to run a factory in China since 1949.

After spending nearly $1 million, Coca-Cola saw its first plant go into production in 1981. "An old comrade in the party's leadership raised another round of concerns," wrote Ma Licheng in his book *Thirty Years of Battle*. "Cannot Chinese drinks meet the needs of the people or foreigners? Must we drink Coca-Cola? This is a blatant act of treason."[19] The "old comrade" demanded an explanation from COFCO, which responded by saying that Coca-Cola products had Chinese ingredients and the distribution of products would be limited.

But it wasn't.

In 1982, Coca began to promote its products in mainstream markets in Beijing. In an effort to change the tastes of the Chinese, who were used to tea and thought Coke tasted like cough medicine, Coca-Cola mounted a campaign that gave out free balloons and chopsticks. Attracted by the giveaways, Chinese customers responded with great enthusiasm. But the promotion backfired when Chinese media launched another round of criticism against Coca-Cola. *Beijing Daily* sent an internal communication to the Politburo Standing Committee of the Chinese Communist Party accusing COFCO of wasting precious foreign currency. Chen Yun, one of the most influential figures in the Politburo, decreed that "not a single bottle of Coke should be sold to Chinese." And overnight, all Coca-Cola products disappeared from shops serving domestic customers. It eventually took Zhao Ziyang, then premier of China and later secretary general of the Communist Party, to lift the injunction and allow Coke to be sold to the Chinese again.

> *In an effort to change the tastes of the Chinese, who were used to tea and thought Coke tasted like cough medicine, Coca-Cola mounted a campaign that gave out free balloons and chopsticks.*

Despite the challenges, Coca-Cola succeeded in the end. China has become Coca-Cola's third largest market in the world, after the United States and Mexico. It has invested over $5 billion in China. More important, Coca-Cola has blazed a trail for other foreign companies—Pepsi, KFC, McDonald's, Coors, Budweiser, IBM, Apple, Dell, Procter & Gamble, Walmart, Sheraton, Hilton, Volkswagen, Ford, General Motors, Boeing, and Airbus. China joined the World Trade Organization (WTO) in 2001, opening its vast market to virtually every business.

By opening its market to foreign businesses, China brought in capital, technology, and talent from the West. Through joint ventures and acquisitions, Western businesses helped transform some of the least productive state-owned companies and private enterprises. Western companies also provided opportunities for Chinese businesses to be part of the global supply chain and thus gain access to the global market. As a result, hundreds of millions of jobs were created. These jobs made it possible for hundreds of millions of peasants to move into factories, restaurants, and shops, alleviating China's population pressure and transforming its vast population from a liability into an asset. These new jobs generated higher income for hundreds of millions of people, increasing their purchasing capacity and enlarging their appetite. Bicycles, wristwatches, and manual sewing machines were the "big three" items in the 1970s, but today the Chinese have become consumers of houses, cars, vacations abroad, French wine, and American universities.

The story of Coca-Cola's return to China is yet another example reminding us that China's economic growth has not been the result of deliberate planning by an authority figure with great foresight. Rather it has been the result of the government's adapting to the demand of the market and people by retreating from planning and regulating. After decades of isolation from the outside world, the Chinese government gradually opened up and allowed foreign business to access its market, resources, and labor force. It has been this opening up, coupled with the autonomy now granted to China's people, that has generated the miraculous growth of the past three decades.

China's economic growth created enough wealth for the government to invest in awe-inspiring skyscrapers, space programs, and infrastructure; advance military technologies; purchase properties and natural resources overseas; and put up spectacular shows such as the 2008 Olympics Games in Beijing and the 2010 World Expo in Shanghai. As a result, the world is experiencing another wave of Sinomania and Sinophobia, four hundred years after the last one.

DÉJÀ VU?

"China is in big trouble," wrote the Nobel laureate economist Paul Krugman in a July 18, 2013, op-ed piece in the *New York Times*.[20] Krugman believes that China's "whole way of doing business, the economic system that has driven three decades of incredible growth, has reached its limits," calling the "China model" into question. "You could say that the Chinese model is about to hit its Great Wall, and the only question now is just how bad the crash will be."

Krugman is not the only one to begin questioning the China model. After China's economic growth rate slowed, for the first time in three decades, to 7.5 percent in 2012, Michael Schuman wrote in *Time*, "The recent slowdown is not a temporary cyclical blip or solely the knockoff effect of the tepid global recovery. China's growth model is broken and can't be so easily fixed."[21]

Some think this is just a temporary slowdown and the Chinese economy will continue to grow. Stephen Leeb, author of *Red Alert: How China's Growing Prosperity Threatens the American Way of Life*, believes Paul Krugman is wrong in his prediction about China in the same way he was wrong about Singapore before. In a July 27, 2013, *Forbes* blog post, Leeb pointed out that Krugman predicted the end of rapid growth in Singapore and other Asian economies such as South Korea, Taiwan, and Hong Kong. "Of course, things did not work out that way," wrote Leeb. "Singapore and the other Asian nations have since grown voluminously." Leeb thinks "what Krugman and many others missed was the foundation for much higher productivity, and indeed Singapore has since proven second to none in leveraging the advantages of modern technology." He argues that today's China, like Singapore twenty years ago, "houses many productivity drivers." One of them is urbanization, which "promises their populace greater education" and "should also strongly drive up productivity and efficiency, as will the vast majority of Chinese infrastructure spending."[22]

The Chinese government showed its appreciation for Leeb's message by placing a Chinese version of the blog in a prominent place on its state-run Xinhua news agency's home page. In an effort to instill confidence in its people, the Chinese government acknowledged the slowdown but promoted it as a deliberate action. "The slowdown is natural," announced Xinhua, in response to a report of slow growth for seven consecutive quarters since 2012, reported by the Chinese Statistics Bureau in July 2013.[23] "In fact the slowdown is an intentional policy choice of the Chinese government," continued Xinhua. "The policy makers are keenly aware that only when freed from the psychological shackles of 'GDP only' and focusing on structural adjustment and further reforms will the Chinese economy be able to move to a higher level." "No one believes that the Chinese economy will have a hard landing," said Chinese Minister of Finance Lou Jiwei in an interview with Xinhua in July 2013.[24]

"The statistics show that the growth rate of Chinese economy is gently slowing down, at 7.9% at the end of last year, 7.7% in the first quarter of this year, and 7.5% in the second quarter," Xinhua declared in another article the same month. "This means the slowdown of the Chinese economy is intentional, gradual, steady, and anticipated."[25]

Whether it is intentional or inevitable, it has happened. The Chinese economy has slowed down. This slowdown, however interpreted, indicates the end of an era for China. The Chinese leadership installed in March 2013 has decided to work on an "upgraded model" instead of fixing the old one. Premier Li Keqiang has made it clear that the government would not provide short-term stimulus to avert the slowdown. Instead, China has adopted a series of policies that have become known as *Likonomics*, a portmanteau of Chinese premier Li Keqiang's name and "economics." (The construction parallels "Reaganomics," coined to refer to the economic policies of President Ronald Reagan.) Likonomics aims to bring more economic structural reforms, reducing governmental interference and increasing urbanization.[26]

The Chinese government's active pursuit of an upgraded model declares the current inadequacy of the old model that fueled China's growth and was admired by so many outsiders. While the old model has indeed brought China thirty years of high-speed growth, it has reached its limit and must be replaced. "If China's economy can be said to have gone through the 'Bronze Age' and 'Silver Age' over the last thirty some years," noted a widely circulated article in the state-run *Shanghai Securities News* in July 2013, "today's new leadership is working hard to create an upgraded model to usher in a brand new 'Golden Age' driven by innovation."[27]

Innovation is what's missing from the old model. China's economic rebirth was the result of the same scenario that made China the number one empire before the Industrial Revolution: a large population left alone by an autocratic government. China grew fast by offering the world the least expensive and most compliant and motivated workforce. But now the population is

shrinking and labor costs
are on the rise. Population
dividends are drying up.
Low-level jobs that once
enriched China are leaving
for countries with even less
expensive labor, such as
Vietnam. It is thus no surprise that China's new leadership has decided to pursue
an innovation-driven eco-
nomic model.

China grew fast by offering the world the least expensive and most compliant and motivated workforce. But now the population is shrinking and labor costs are on the rise.

Zhen Haixiong, deputy
chief editor of Xinhua, sum-
marized China's urgent need for moving toward an economy
driven by innovation in the July 29, 2013, issue of *Outlook Weekly*,
the agency's official news magazine:

> After over thirty years of rapid development, our nation has made
> enviable progress and certainly become the world's second largest
> economy. In the meantime, a number of problems have become
> increasingly prominent and unavoidable: unbalanced structure, low
> productivity and efficiency, rising labor costs, limited energy and
> resources, and constraints of the environment. These problems
> suggest that the traditional model of development cannot continue.
> The decisive battle for China's near and long term development is
> to focus our major efforts on scientific and technological
> innovations and realize the innovation-driven development
> strategy.[28]

But innovation does not come easily. It does not come simply
as a result of economic policies or the desires of a government.
It comes from creative individuals. Can China's education produce
such individuals?

4

HESITANT LEARNER
The Struggle of Halfway Westernization

Shanghai—August 11, 1872. Thirty teenage boys bid tearful good-byes to their families and friends. Cheered by the crowd onshore, their loved ones waving hands as the ship sailed out of port, the boys began their month-long journey to the United States. They were the first of four groups of students sent by the Qing imperial government to study in the United States. Through the Chinese Educational Mission (CEM) program, 120 boys aged eleven through fifteen would study in America for fifteen years. The Chinese government would pay for all of their living and educational expenses, with the expectation that they would return to work for the government. This was one of China's many efforts to acquire Western technology and strengthen itself in the face of Western aggression. The plan was conceived and brought to fruition by Yung Wing, a Yale graduate and the first Chinese to graduate from any Western university. He was convinced that Western education would enlighten, empower, and reenergize his homeland.

Shanghai—September 7, 1881. A large crowd gathered at the wharf, all eyes on the approaching boat. It docked, and off came the first group of boys who had sailed to America a decade earlier. Now confident young men, they scanned the crowd for their parents, relatives, and friends, but they had no time to find them. Instead of the warm welcome they'd been imagining, they were met by armed guards who swiftly had them carted away in wheelbarrows to an abandoned school building. Along the way, they were jeered and mocked as "foreign devils." They were kept in the damp, filthy, pest-ridden building for days and forbidden to see their families. Instead of being embraced with open arms by their motherland and entering government to help China become enlightened and powerful, they were interrogated, then assigned to low-level jobs and paid a coolie's wage. In the eyes of their fellow countrymen and the officials who had sent them to the United States, they returned not as heroic patriots but as suspicious traitors who would need to be closely monitored.[1]

> *They returned not as heroic patriots but as suspicious traitors who would need to be closely monitored.*

The boys' early return had not been their decision. A month earlier, the Qing government had cut short their fifteen-year study plan. A few weeks later, the rest of 120 boys came back to China—except for a few who had been expelled from the program, had died, or had escaped being sent back.

A GRAND EXPERIMENT

The boys weren't called home because they had completed their planned study; only three had graduated from college by 1881, and most of the others were still in high school or college. They weren't called back because they couldn't handle living in America. Quite to the contrary; they had quickly adapted to their new living environment, and many quite enjoyed their life in America. They had not failed academically; in fact, all of the boys had excellent academic records and exhibited great potential. Their work was shown at the Philadelphia Centennial Exposition in 1876 and received high praise—even from President Grant and the First

Lady, who made a point of meeting the boys and shaking their hands. The scholars' return wasn't even connected to the anti-Chinese sentiment that was spreading across the United States. The boys had been warmly welcomed by their host families and the media. When Congress passed the Chinese Exclusion Act in 1882 in response to rising concerns about the influx of Chinese laborers, the Chinese Educational Mission participants were not affected.

No, the reason for terminating the program was that these boys were becoming more than what the Qing imperial court had planned for them. While Yung Wing, the Yale graduate who instigated the plan, might have had the idea that they would return with enlightened minds to help rejuvenate the old empire, the government officials and emperor wanted them to learn only military and technical skills. After all, technology seemed the only thing the oldest empire was missing—and the only thing worth learning from the youngest republic. The ancient Chinese civilization had an infinitely superior culture and far more refined ways of living. The Qing officials wanted these boys to stay as far away from the barbaric American culture as possible.

The Qing officials wanted these boys to stay as far away from the barbaric American culture as possible.

But the boys did not, could not, stay away from American culture. They were immersed in it. Upon arrival, they were placed in pairs in about sixty families in the New England area, mostly around Hartford, Connecticut. These families had been recruited with the help of Birdsey Grant Northrop, secretary of the Connecticut State Board of Education, who had circulated a letter to churches throughout Connecticut and Massachusetts. The host families were generally well educated, deeply religious, and well respected in their communities. They brought the boys to church and social events and treated them as adoptive children, giving them the same support and discipline they gave their own children. Some of the boys attended public high schools, while others went to private academies, but all were exposed to a Western curriculum and to extracurricular athletics and social events.

To counter "the seductive influence of foreign learning," the Chinese government prescribed a course of Chinese studies for the boys.[2] During the school year, one hour of each day was devoted to the study of Chinese. Every three months, the boys were required to travel to Hartford, where the mission was headquartered, and spend two weeks taking intensive courses devoted to the memorization and recitation of the classics, Chinese composition, and calligraphy. In summers, they spent six weeks taking these intensive courses in Hartford. On certain days, calculated by the Chinese calendar, the boys were required to participate in rituals designed to remind them of their Chinese identity and impart the rules a Confucian scholar must follow. They were also required to hear the commissioner read Emperor Kangxi's "Sacred Edict" and to perform ceremonial obeisance to the emperor.

But the Chinese studies and rituals weren't powerful enough to keep the boys away from American ways of thinking and living. First, the boys took a liking to sports—something a good Confucian scholar would never do. Not only did the Chinese boys enjoy baseball, football, and hockey, but they played them brilliantly. A small group of boys even formed their own baseball team and called it the Orientals. They won a game against an Oakland team right before they returned to China.[3]

The boys were also popular at school dances and had no problem finding partners of the opposite sex. Because their braided queues were inconvenient for sports and sometimes cause for ridicule in social settings, most of the boys hid them inside their hats or shirts, and a few brave ones cut them off, a sign of disloyalty in the Qing dynasty. Gradually the boys began to assume a Western identity. When Sze Kin Yung had visiting cards printed, for example, he changed his name to "Sydney C. Shih." He also participated in church activities, exchanged letters with a female schoolmate, and socialized with other girls. Worst of all, some of the boys converted to Christianity. One student showed reluctance to bow to the Confucian tablet, and another cut off his queue and announced his decision to become Christian in a letter to his father. A few students even formed a group called Chinese Christian Home Mission, hoping to convert the whole of China to Christ.

The Qing officials were deeply concerned, and often enraged, by these changes in the boys. The most serious offenders were expelled from the mission and ordered to return to China (although some got away and stayed in the United States). But the Chinese government continued to hope that the others would finish their studies and maintain their Chinese heritage.

In January 1880, the mission's fourth and final commissioner, Woo Tse Tun, published an open letter in the *Hartford Daily Courant* in which he urged the boys to study hard and never forget their Chinese tradition. Woo reminded the boys of the great sacrifices their government and parents had made to support their study, "the hope of both country and parents being that; for a lifetime you may, on the one hand recompense the state by your services, and on the other that you may bring honor to your ancestor." Woo urged the boys "not to neglect the rules of etiquette... If you deliberately neglect all the rules of politeness of your native country, on your return home, how can you live in sympathy with your fellow countrymen?" Woo warned the students that "foreign habits should not become so rooted as that you cannot change them."[4] His language was mild, but his choice of a public forum in which to lecture the boys showed the significance of the issue. And the language he used in his report to the Qing officials was not nearly as mild:

The boys love American sports just like the Americans. They spend
more time on sports than on studying. Moreover they follow the
example of the Americans and joined all sorts of secret societies,
some of them religious and others political, but all engaged in
improper conducts. Thus they show no respect for teachers and do
not follow our lectures. Furthermore most of the students have
converted to Christianity because of studying Christian sciences or
attending Sunday schools. If we let these students stay in America
for long they will no doubt lose their love for their motherland.
Even if they eventually complete their study and return to China,
the boys will be of no particular value to the country. Instead they
will bring harm to the society. For the sake of the happiness of
China, we should immediately disband the mission and recall all
students. If the plan is acted upon one day earlier, it gives China
good fortune one day earlier.[5]

Yung Wing was sympathetic to the students and had in fact
wanted them to become more Westernized. However, he was
only the deputy commissioner—and the fact that he was never
given the commissioner position showed the Qing government's
lack of trust in him, no doubt because of his Westernized identity.
Wing's marriage to an American woman gave the government
even more cause to be wary. As a result, he had little power, and
he wasn't well connected to the Qing court officials. News and
reports of the commission's progress came from the more conservative commissioners. And these reports made it almost impossible for the early supporters to defend the mission.

Furthermore, Yung's application to the State Department to
allow the students to be enrolled at the Military Academy in West
Point and the Naval Academy in Annapolis had been denied.
Therefore, one of the primary goals of sending the boys to the
United States—to acquire military skills and technology—could
not be accomplished. In addition, the rise in commodity prices
led to a request for increased funding, which opened a debate
about the program's usefulness.

Members of the Qing court decided that their investment was not going to result in what they wanted: loyal and obedient technicians. Instead, these boys' education was making them independent thinkers and defiant individuals who could pose a threat to the existing imperial order. Yung Wing rallied support, including a joint petition by Mark Twain, Yale president Noah Porter, and Amherst College president Julius Seelye to the Chinese Bureau of Foreign Affairs, praising the students for their progress and good behavior and strongly urging the Chinese government to let the boys complete their planned study. Even President Ulysses Grant tried to rescue the program by sending a personal appeal to his friend Governor Li Hongzhang, the original supporter of the program in the Qing court. But Governor Li was outranked by Prince Gong, head of the Bureau of Foreign Affairs and uncle of the reigning emperor, who favored terminating the program.

On June 8, 1881, the students began their journey back to China.

WISHFUL THINKING

The fate of the CEM exemplifies China's journey to modernization and innovation over the last century and a half. At first, the Chinese elites were reluctant to accept any need for change. As Confucian scholars, they believed that China possessed a superior culture, and every rule and principle needed for a great civilization had already been discovered and prescribed by ancient "saints"—Confucius and his followers. China's military defeats and apparent weakness were simply the result of failing to follow these rules and principles. The way to gain strength was to restore the ancient rules and principles, not make innovative changes. "The idealistic picture of this era envisions a genuine conservative effort at a 'Restoration' similar to those that had occurred after the founding of the Later Han or after the great mid-Tang rebellion," write historians John Fairbank and Merle Goldman about China's actions in the 1860s.[6]

But the "restoration" failed. A few influential officials in the Qing imperial court began to realize that "the foreigners' domination of China was based on the superiority of their weapons, that it was hopeless to try to drive them out, and that Chinese society therefore faced the greatest crisis since its unification under the First Emperor in 221 B.C."[7] China realized the need to train its people to use Western machinery to strengthen itself against the West. This reasoning led to the Self-Strengthening Movement, a series of programs, including the CEM, to bring in Western technologies and allow a few Chinese to learn Western machinery.

But accepting the need to learn Western machinery meant just that: the West had superior machinery, but nothing else. Following the attractive but fallacious doctrine of "Chinese learning as the foundation, Western learning as the utility," China began to purchase weapons and gunboats. But direct importation became costly and inconvenient, so China decided to import the technology it needed to manufacture these machines inside China. To staff the factories and operate the machines, China also imported training by both bringing foreign experts in and sending Chinese overseas.

All of these efforts were conducted with the understanding that all that China needed to learn from the West was technology— the low-level, technical stuff unworthy of the attention of well-educated Confucian scholars and officials. Western learning was generally looked down on. For example, although hundreds of Western works in science and technology had been translated into Chinese, the Chinese scholars showed little interest in them. As a result, the print runs were small, and the materials barely circulated among Chinese scholars.

An even more telling example is the uproar surrounding Tong Wen Guan, generally considered the first modern institute of higher learning in China. It was established in 1862, by the same department that administered the CEM, to train interpreters to deal with the many treaties and increased presence of foreigners. The school first offered training in English and then added French, Russian, German, and Japanese. In 1866, Prince Gong suggested the addition of a department to teach Western sciences, which triggered a wave of angry reactions from the conservative elites and bureaucrats. Grand Secretary of the Qing court Wo Ren wrote in a memorial to the throne: "The root of a country is the morals of the people, not technology. Now we begin to seek the branch of technology [instead of the root of moral] and make foreigners our teacher...and force our smartest and best educated to learn from foreigners. Consequently the right is suppressed and the wrong gets to spread. In a few years, all Chinese will follow foreigners."[8]

Yang Tingxi, governor of Zhili Province (today's Hebei Province), even blamed the drought in the summer of 1867 on the establishment of Tong Wen Guan and called it a warning sign from heaven. He suggested immediate dissolution of the institute so as to appease heaven. Because of the negative attitude toward Western knowledge, Tong Wen Guan had great difficult recruiting quality students. The government had to pay students a salary to study there and promise immediate appointment to the official ranks on graduation. In the beginning, Tong Wen Guan had only students who could not achieve success in the *keju* exams or who desperately needed the money. The CEM had the same problem in recruiting students: no decent families wanted their children to study Western knowledge or learn from Western teachers.

The Chinese government did not want to acquire Western technology at the expense of cultural stability. The quest for innovation had to proceed with great caution so as to avoid contaminating the minds of the Chinese with Western values, sacrificing the Chinese civilization, and destabilizing the existing order. In all efforts to acquire Western technology, China took the utmost care to separate the technology from its surrounding culture.

However, historical evidence suggests that such separation was wishful thinking. It was simply delusional to believe that "Western arms, steamships, science, and technology could somehow be utilized to preserve Confucian values," observe Fairbank and Goldman. "In retrospect we can see that gunboats and steel mills bring their own philosophy with them."[9]

Purchasing navy fleets from the West did not help China win more wars; the Sino-Japanese wars proved that. In 1894, China had the best-equipped navy in Asia yet was defeated by Japan, which had technologically inferior ships but had Westernized its political, societal, military, and industrial institutions with the Meiji Restoration, a series of political and social reforms that spanned 1868 to 1912. China had tried to extract Western technology from the culture in which it was embedded, and as a result, the technology failed to make China more powerful, as the Self-Strengthening Movement soon showed. It was also impossible to learn technical skills from the West without learning Western culture, as the CEM had demonstrated.

Many of China's conservative scholars realized the folly of trying to Westernize by halfway measures. But the West's technology, science, and military power—not to mention the material wealth that technology and science brought—grew even more irresistible as time went on. The West could not simply be ignored nor could its influence be kept out by closing all borders or building a great wall as previous emperors had. Despite opposition from its own scholars, China had to engage with the West in all sorts of ways on its journey toward modernization. In the end, China "was sucked into an inexorable process in which one borrowing led to another," Fairbank and Goldman reflect, "from machinery to technology, from science to all learning, from acceptance of new ideas to change of institutions, eventually from constitutional reform to republican revolution."[10]

Institutional changes and republican revolution did not settle China's ideological dispute about the West, though. Dramatic as those changes were, they did not alter China's imperial way of thinking. The Republic of China was in no way a Western-style democracy. Yuan Shikai, the second president of the Republic, wanted to turn the country back into an empire just four years after its establishment. The Qing emperor was restored, albeit for only twelve days, in 1917—six years after the founding of the Republic. The Republic was then effectively governed by Chiang Kai-shek, who ruled as an emperor (although he was himself a devoted Christian until his death in 1975). He passed the presidency of a much reduced Republic of China (essentially Taiwan and its neighboring islands) to his son, Chiang Ching-kuo, who ruled until his death in 1988.

On the mainland, the Communist Party took control of the country, bundling Chinese imperial thinking into a Western ideology invented by a German, Karl Marx. The People's Republic of China came under the control of Mao Zedong, who had deep knowledge of Chinese tradition and learning but no direct experience with the West. Although he led multiple campaigns against the Confucian tradition, Mao was a devoted admirer of the first emperor, Qin Shi Huang, who had unified China two thousand years before. He promoted historic Chinese rebels who changed dynasties and replaced emperors. In terms of his supremacy, Mao was no different from "a monarch in succession to scores of emperors" in China. In their book *China: A New History*, Fairbank and Goldman called him "an updated emperor."[11]

Under Mao's autocratic rule, China went back to being an empire closed off to the outside world. As in previous empires, maintaining control of the people was of paramount importance. Although technology and science were acknowledged to be necessary for economic development, they would be sacrificed if they became a threat to maintaining control. Seeing the destabilizing effect of Western ideas, Mao followed the conservative scholars of the late Qing dynasty and opposed anything foreign. "We'd rather have socialist weed than capitalist seedlings" was a popular slogan during the Cultural Revolution from 1966 to 1976, meaning China would rather have socialist ignorance than capitalist knowledge. As a result, Western-educated intellectuals were considered "traitors" and had to be reeducated.[12] Western books were banned, and listening to the Voice of America was considered a crime. People with overseas ties were put under surveillance as possible spies. "Foreign imperialism was ended but so were foreign stimuli, while old 'feudal' [traditional] values and corrupt practices remained still embedded in Chinese society."[13]

> *Western-educated intellectuals were considered "traitors" and had to be reeducated.*

SELF-STRENGTHENING MOVEMENT VERSION 2.0

Cut off from Western technology and science, Mao formed his own ideas of technological and scientific innovation—and they all proved disastrous. For example, in November 1957, he decided that China should surpass Britain, the United States, and other industrial countries in ten to fifteen years, and he believed that the amount of steel a nation produced was the correct measure of its strength. So to meet his goal, the Communist Party decided in 1958 that China should produce 10.7 million tons of steel and called on the whole country to participate. All of China was suddenly engaged in steelmaking. Millions of backyard iron smelters were set up all over the country—in cornfields, on hilltops, in courtyards, and literally in backyards. More than 100 million people—one in every six Chinese—took part in this campaign without possessing either the knowledge or the proper equipment necessary to make steel. In December 1958, after the melting of millions of cooking pots and other iron objects, China's government announced that the country had produced 11.08 tons of steel, exceeding its goal twelve days ahead of schedule. Alas, only 8 million tons of the steel were usable. The estimated damage was over 20 billion RMB, or about one-sixth of China's GDP in 1958.

Mao's ideas about agriculture were even more damaging. To please the Great Leader and Helmsman and prove him correct, Chinese peasants entered into a national contest of grain production measured by the amount of grains harvested per *mu* (0.164 acres). The *People's Daily*, the national state-run newspaper, published a regularly updated league table of the best harvesting record. On June 8, 1958, a village in Henan reported harvesting 2,015 *jin* (about 2,216 pounds) of wheat per *mu*. This record was smashed a day later by a commune in Hubei with 2,357 *jin* (2,592 pounds). The record was broken every few days, and by the time the year ended, the top harvest had reached 8,585 *jin* (9,440 pounds). Although these numbers are perhaps one hundred times greater than what was actually harvested and violated both science and common sense, Mao and his loyal followers did not begin to doubt them until a few years later. Instead, Mao reportedly worried about what the peasants would do with so much food and suggested they have five meals a day. The reality, within a few years, was massive starvation.

Mao died in 1976, just as China was about to collapse. His successors, led by Deng Xiaoping, decided that China indeed needed Western technology and science. Deng had traveled to France at the age of sixteen under a work-study program and stayed there for four years, until he was sent to the Soviet Union in 1926. When he returned to China and rose to leadership, he made massive changes under the slogan of "reform and opening up to the outside world."

The "reform," as discussed in chapter 3, consisted mostly of granting more autonomy to China's citizens and withdrawing governmental control from their daily lives. The "opening up" meant reengaging with the outside world—mostly the West. A century earlier, China had been forced, by guns and cannons, to open its eyes to the West. This time, the opening was China's own decision. Not everyone was in favor, and only a leader with absolute authority could have made such a decision. It was Deng Xiaoping, China's de facto emperor at the time, who announced that China must end its isolation from the rest of the world.

June 23, 1978, was a grand milestone on China's journey toward modernization, for on that day, Deng Xiaoping issued the decree to send Chinese to study overseas. At a meeting with the leadership of Tsinghua University (founded in 1911 to prepare students to study in US universities under the Boxer Indemnity Scholarship Program),[14] Deng said, "I agree that we should send more people to study abroad, mostly in natural sciences. Let's send tens of thousands, instead of eight or ten...This is one of the important ways to rapidly improve our science and education in five years."[15] Deng asked the Ministry of Education to come up with a plan, adding, "Regardless of the costs, it's worth it." What was even more remarkable was Deng's liberal view about management of the students. Officials at the Ministry of Education were understandably deeply worried that students might defect. But Deng told them not to isolate the students from their hosting society, because they should learn not only science and technology but also about foreign societies.

Within two months, the Ministry of Education had a plan ready. In October, a Chinese delegation was dispatched to Washington, DC, to negotiate with the US government. The negotiations were not easy, since the two countries did not have a diplomatic relationship, but eventually it was agreed that the United States would accept between five hundred and seven hundred Chinese students and scholars, and the United States would send sixty students and scholars to China in 1978–1979. On December 26, 1978, just in time for the historic visit of Deng

Xiaoping to the United States in January 1979, fifty-two Chinese students and scholars arrived in New York via Paris.

At the same time, China began to bring in foreign experts and investment. Foreign machinery and technology were imported to help with modernization, and foreign companies were gradually allowed to enter China. The events of the late 1970s and early 1980s were much like the Self-Strengthening Movement one hundred years earlier—similar attempts to borrow and learn from the West, with the same goal of acquiring Western technology without Western culture. For example, to prevent potential contamination, foreigners were allowed to stay only in government-designated hotels or guarded houses and could not visit ordinary Chinese homes without proper authorization. Chinese had to obtain permission to interact with foreigners in private.

History repeats itself: what had been impossible one hundred years earlier remained impossible. As China opened its door to Western technology and science, Western ideas streamed in. No matter how hard China's leaders worked to separate the Chinese from foreign people and ideas, Western values and lifestyles began to spread, and Western arts, music, and fashion found their way into Chinese society.

> *No matter how hard China's leaders worked to separate the Chinese from foreign people and ideas, Western values and lifestyles began to spread.*

Meanwhile, a few courageous intellectuals began to deliberately introduce Western ideas and knowledge about the West. In 1980, Zhong Shuhe, once imprisoned for liberal ideas during the Cultural Revolution, persuaded *Hunan People's Press* to republish writings of late Qing dynasty scholars and officials about Western countries. These writings came out as a series of books under the title *From East to West: Chinese Travellers before 1911*, bringing an old West to China through the eyes of liberal scholars. That series retained some shock value, but even more impact came from another collection of writings, *Series into the Future*. Conceived and organized by a group of young intellectuals (no one on the editorial board was over forty-five years old), this series focused on more contemporary development of both social and natural sciences. It included original writings of Chinese scholars and translated Western works such as Douglas Hofstadter's *Gödel, Escher, Bach: An Eternal Golden Braid* and *The Limits to Growth*, commissioned by the Club of Rome. Fashioned after the Bibliothèque Bleue during the French Enlightenment, the overarching goal of the series was to "help enlighten people, promote universal values, and modernize China in all aspects," said its chief editor, Jing Guanta, in an interview twenty years later.[16]

But like their counterparts one hundred years earlier, the conservatives of the late twentieth century resisted the influx of Western ideas and culture. They took action, launching a series of campaigns against the importation of Western ideas. In 1983, party conservatives began the Anti-Spiritual Pollution campaign to curb the spread of Western culture and ideas. Spiritual pollution was said to have many symptoms, and its contamination could be seen in works that promoted humanism: films, theater, music, and dance from the West (including Taiwan and Hong Kong); Western hairstyles (curly, colored, or, for men, long); Western clothing (e.g., jeans); and facial hair. The campaign was not popular; it reminded people a little too sharply of the Cultural Revolution. Deng Xiaoping intervened, ending the campaign after two months.

The resistance did not go away as easily. In early 1987, another campaign was launched against "bourgeois liberalization," following a stern speech by the very leader who opened China to the world, Deng Xiaoping. "The purpose of implementing the open policies was to learn foreign technology and utilize foreign investments," said Deng at a private meeting with top leaders of the Communist Party on December 30, 1986. "It is to improve socialist construction, but we cannot deviate from the socialist path...We talk about democracy, but we cannot copy capitalist democracy. We cannot have the three-branch government." Deng brought America directly into the conversation: "I have always criticized American leaders and said they have three governments... Certainly the capitalist America can use this to trick other countries but their internal fights give them lots of problems. We cannot adopt this scheme." In his speech, he called for the persecution of a few scientists and scholars for their liberal views.[17]

Less than three weeks after Deng's speech, Hu Yaobang, who had held the top position of the Communist Party since 1982, was forced to resign as the party secretary general. The reason given was that he had not opposed bourgeois liberalization forcefully enough. Once again, the influx of Western ideas had led to the questioning of Chinese tradition and current authority figures.

Although earlier attempts to introduce Western ideas had caused concerns and reactions from the conservative Communist leaders, the resistance campaigns were short and limited in scope. It took a popular TV documentary, with its direct and explicit negation of the value of Chinese tradition, to bring about harsh retaliation and a full crackdown. In 1988, the Chinese Central TV (CCTV) station, the state-run national TV network, broadcast a six-part documentary entitled *River Elegy*. The gist of the historical documentary was that China's ancient, land-based civilization was conducive to despotism and feudalism. As a result, the Chinese tended to accept authority, be inward looking, and lack an adventurous spirit—just the opposite of ocean-faring Europeans and Americans. The color yellow, a proud Chinese symbol for thousands of years, was cast as a symbol of backwardness, ignorance, and submission to tyranny. The three symbols of the Chinese civilization—the Yellow River, the dragon, and the Great Wall—were reinterpreted as symbols of tyranny and isolationism. Most damaging was the conclusion:

> This yellow land cannot teach us what true scientific spirit means.

> The tyrannical Yellow River cannot teach us what true democracy is.

> This yellow land and river can no longer support a rapidly growing population nor can it breed a new culture. It has lost its nutrition and energy.

> The Confucian culture may have some perfect magic in the past, but for thousands of years, it has not cultivated the entrepreneurial spirit a people should have, the legal order a country needs, or a renewal mechanism a culture must have. Instead, in its decline, the Confucian culture never stops destroying its best, killing its enlivening elements, and suffocating the nation's talents generation after generation.[18]

The conclusion was that the Yellow River was dead (hence the film's title). For renewal, China had to look for ideas in Western culture—civilizations based on blue oceans.

River Elegy became an instant national phenomenon. More than 200 million viewers watched the documentary, which became the hottest topic of conversation on college campuses, in offices, and at gatherings of intellectuals. Clubs, forums, and seminars were founded all over the country specifically to discuss this film. Its script was published in *People's Daily* and more than ten other newspapers, and four publishing houses printed the script as a monograph. CCTV set a precedent by broadcasting the film in prime time twice in two months. Zhao Ziyang, who succeeded Hu Yaobang as secretary general of the Communist Party was said to have given copies of the film to leaders of Singapore. The film also reached Japan and became popular among its intellectuals.

River Elegy did not flow unnoticed past the conservatives of the Communist Party. Wang Zhen, a decorated Communist general who had joined the party at the age of fourteen back in 1927, led a campaign against the documentary. China's newly elected vice president was infuriated by the film, and he swiftly gathered like-minded comrades to publicly denounce it. In September 1988, Wang summoned the chief editor of *People's Daily* to his home and said angrily, "We cannot put up with this anymore." On September 30, at a high-level meeting of the party, Wang made an emotional speech calling for action. On October 8, the Chinese government banned the film. It could no longer be shown in China, let alone exported to other countries.[19]

But the worst was yet to come for *River Elegy* and its makers. After the government's crackdown on massive protests in Tiananmen Square, *River Elegy* was charged with planting the seed for the June 1989 student demonstration and serving as "a blueprint of a counter-revolution" to end Communist rule and bring in capitalist liberalization. Zhao Ziyang was sacked as party general secretary and put under house arrest for supporting capitalist liberation. As evidence, he was accused of ordering the making and national distribution of the film. But according to one of its primary authors, Su Xiaokang, the accusation was a complete fabrication. "I am a writer. I have no association with politics. I never met Bao Tong or Chen Yizhi, let alone Zhao Ziyang," said Su in an interview with the Independent Chinese Pen Center, a nonprofit organization for Chinese authors in exile.[20]

The lead authors of the film escaped punishment by either hiding in China or going into exile in the United States. The Chinese government organized a massive campaign to denounce the film in media and among intellectuals in the aftermath of the Tiananmen demonstration. Under the banner of antipeaceful evolution and against all-out Westernization, all liberal ideas were suppressed. Journals and newspapers that had published liberal ideas were shut down or had their editorial teams sacked. The once popular "enlightenment" series was banned and its publications discontinued. Their leading editors and authors were removed from their jobs or went into exile.

The modern Self-Strengthening Movement ended just as the previous one had. Seeing the destabilizing power of Western ideas and the successive collapse of former Communist regimes in Eastern Europe in 1989 and 1990, the Chinese Communist Party decided that China had experienced too much reform. For the next three years, China would focus on cleaning up Western contamination.

HARMONY AND INNOVATION

By the time China started its modern decontamination project, the world had changed. The 1990s were very different from the 1890s: China could not simply put itself back into isolation. Like it or not, the country had to continue its economic development. In January 1992, Deng Xiaoping came out of retirement and took a month-long trip. He visited some of the most important cities in the southern provinces, particularly Guangdong, the first major province to experiment with his reforms and engage with the outside world. Deng made a number of speeches reaffirming his vision of "reform and opening up." Although retired, he retained a monarch's power. His speeches forced China's leader, Jiang Zemin, to restart economic reforms and engage with foreign countries.

The next twenty years saw rapid economic growth and broader interactions with the West. In 2001, China became a member of the World Trade Organization, officially joining the global economy. Western things no longer look strange in China's landscape. McDonald's, KFC, and Coca-Cola are household names in China. Ford, General Motors, and Toyota cars clog Chinese streets. Western musicians perform in Chinese theaters and bars. In 2013,

Celine Dion performed for the Chinese on CCTV's most celebrated program, *Chinese Spring Festival Evening*. Almost half of the Chinese people, about 600 million, now use the Internet. Foreigners are free to travel in China and can choose to stay anywhere they like; they can befriend—or marry—any Chinese. Nearly half a million Chinese students studied abroad in 2012, about 200,000 of them in America. In 2013, the Chinese are expected to make over 900 million overseas trips. New York University began to enroll students on its Shanghai campus in 2013, and many other universities are opening campuses in China.

Much has changed, but only on the periphery. China remains China at its core. The Confucian tradition runs deep, and the government remains adamantly opposed to Western forms of government and cultural values. In fact, with its newly accumulated wealth and thirty years of miraculous economic growth, China has gained the confidence to once again assert that it has a superior culture and form of government. An article published in the *Qiushi* (*Hongqi Wengao*) magazine of the Central Committee of the Chinese Communist Party in March 2013 argues that the Chinese political system is the best of the world. Rather than basing this claim on Marxist doctrines, the author points to *Shanran*, an ancient practice of power transition in China:[21]

> The mechanism of power change at the highest level in China today has the characteristics of the "Shanran" tradition but it removes the limitation of life-long occupancy through one-party rule, national selection, long-time cultivation, age-limit, and term-limit...This model basically combines the merits of the Western and Arabic systems and avoids their problems. One-party rule can avoid the risks of the contracted agents and enable long-term strategic planning. National selection and long-term cultivation maximizes the ability to identify the best talent and thus avoid mediocre leaders resulted from democracy. Term-limits enable an influx of new blood, eliminating he risk of having political strongmen.[22]

The article expresses what the Communist leadership has in mind, which is what the Qing emperors and their scholar-officials wanted: the innovations that brought the West technological and scientific advancement, combined with the authoritarian political system and culture that have been the tradition of China. The concept of "harmony and innovation" originates with Hu Jintao, who was China's top leader from 2002 to 2012. The concept is no more than a fresh package for the same content that has dominated China's thinking since 1840. "Harmony and innovation" has proven to be an impossible combination.

In the future, China needs to move to a new stage, one where it can innovate rather than simply borrow or improve on existing technology.

China's 150-year quest for modernization has been a frustrating one because using Western technology to defend the Confucian tradition didn't work well. When Western culture was kept out, so was Western technology. When Western technology came in, so did Western culture. In the future, China needs to move to a new stage, one where it can innovate rather than simply borrow or improve on existing technology. Can Confucian harmony breed Western innovation?

5

FOOLING THE EMPEROR
The Truth about China's Capacity for Innovation

It came down like pink snow falling from the sky," one witness said. "Like pink butterflies," suggested children playing in their Beijing backyards. "They came down and landed everywhere, the lawn, the flower bed, and bushes."

As it turned out, the "pink snow" or "pink butterflies" that floated to earth on September 1, 2013, were three thousand pink hundred-yuan bills with Chairman Mao's portrait on them. The 300,000 RMB (about $50,000) were thrown out of the window of a fifteenth-floor apartment during a police raid. Dressed as workers from a gas company, police officers had raided a fake publishing ring, giving them no time to hide their profits.[1]

Led by a young man and his wife, this group of seven offered to publish scientific papers in their fake medical science journals for fees ranging from 2,000 to 4,000 RMB. Thousands of medical professionals from more than twenty provinces had sent in their payments and had their papers published. In some cases, the ring also offered to write the papers. The three thousand pink butterflies were just a fraction of the millions the ring had received since the start of their operation in 2009.

The ringleader, identified by his family name, Li, was a twenty-seven-year-old high school graduate. He was a good writer, and at first he'd made a living by ghost-writing research papers. But his ambitions exceeded the pay. He ventured into a far more profitable business when he realized just how many medical professionals were in desperate need of publications in order to get promoted. Li found partners and established a bogus press to publish "medical journals." At first, he wrote the papers himself or produced them by copying and pasting from papers he found online. But his business grew so quickly that he couldn't meet the demand. So to increase his stock of papers, he conducted a public contest for the best medical research papers. He then sold the entries and made a handsome profit, completing his transformation from laborer to capitalist entrepreneur.

Academic misconduct and dishonesty exist everywhere, but rarely do they become opportunities to create a billion-dollar industry. A team of researchers led by Sheng Yang, a computer scientist at Wuhan University who develops antiplagiarism software, estimated the fraudulent-publication industry to be worth about 1 billion yuan in 2009.[2] It's a full-service business, ghostwriting academic papers that report the results of fictional research studies as well as getting papers published in both legitimate and not-so-legitimate journals. The team at Wuhan University identified about eight hundred websites dedicated to providing such services. Together they received over 200,000 hits a day, and over three-quarters of those hits came from universities and institutions, according to a 2010 report in the British science journal *Nature*.[3]

THE EMPEROR'S NEW WISHES

The billion-yuan market in fake publishing is a direct result of China's eagerness and determination to rapidly develop its own scientific and technological innovations, actualized in the traditional Chinese-style mass campaign. In the Great Leap Forward and similar mass campaigns, when the emperor (or, more recently, the Chinese central government) desires something, the people make it happen at any cost and in all sorts of ways, including fabrication. Back in 1958, when Chairman Mao wanted China's steel production to surpass that of Western countries, the people made his wish come true. Whether the steel was real or not didn't matter, nor did its quality, just so long as they made enough of it.

When the emperor (or, more recently, the Chinese central government) desires something, the people make it happen, at any cost and in all sorts of ways, including fabrication.

After the Cultural Revolution ended in 1976, Chinese leaders began to acknowledge the power of science and technology. The new mind-set dramatically shifted the role and status of intellectuals, who had been considered dangerous and counterrevolutionary during the Mao era. In 1978, Deng Xiaoping made the obvious (but at the time radical) point that science and technology are forces of productivity. In 1988, he went a step further, calling science and technology the primary forces of productivity. The leaders who followed him all believed that science and technology would drive China's future. Xi Jinping, China's new leader, recently emphasized that innovation must be at the "core of national development."[4] And so to turn China into a nation of innovators, the government set forth highly specific and ambitious goals. In the *National Planning Framework for Long and Short-Range Science and Technology Development* released by the State Council in 2006, China announced that by 2015, it wanted to be one of the top five countries for the number of patents filed and the number of research papers cited.

The emperor can never be disappointed. Lo and behold, the goals have already been achieved, well ahead of schedule. In

2006, China replaced the United Kingdom as the second largest producer of scientific papers published in English, surpassed only by the United States. "China could overtake the United States as the world's dominant publisher of scientific research by 2013," the *Guardian* had noted in 2011, describing a Royal Society study on global trends in scientific research.[5] Sure enough, in September 2013, China became one of the world's top five countries for the number of times its authors' scientific and technology papers were cited.[6] Two years earlier, in 2011, it had become the number one nation for patent applications.[7] And beginning in 2008 and continuing to 2012, it was number three for patents granted, far exceeding its goal to be in the top five by 2015.[8]

China's achievement is even more extraordinary when you consider just how quickly the transformation took place. In 1998, just over 20,000 papers published in journals included in the Science Citation Index (SCI) database were authored by Chinese nationals. A decade later, more than five times that many papers were Chinese, and the total reached 116,000 in 2012. While China's number of SCI papers grew exponentially, most other countries' output remained stable, and the number of US papers grew by about 30 percent. The relative growth of China's number of science papers since the 1980s is stunning. According to a 2009 Thomson Reuters report, if the volume of publications included in the database was 100 in 1981, China's volume would have risen above 5,000 while the total output for the rest of the world, including the United States and the European Union, remained under 500.[9]

> *Chinese patents grew from 12,672 in 1991 to 415,829 in 2011, a thirty-two-fold increase.*

Chinese patents grew just as fast, jumping from 12,672 in 1991 to 415,829 in 2011, a thirty-two-fold increase.[10] In the decade between 2001 and 2011, Chinese patent applications increased by more than thirteen times, from 30,038 to 415,829. The number of patents granted to Chinese residents grew even faster. In 1997, China ranked twelfth in the number of patents granted to residents: 1,532. That number increased by more seventy-three times, rising to 112,347 in 2011.

THE MIRACLE MAKERS

China has delivered a miracle. The sheer number of its patents and frequency of its paper citations in recent years—not to mention the rate of its growth—are awe inspiring. And the miracle becomes even more extraordinary when you consider its makers.

An advanced degree is not required for conducting scientific research and publishing research papers or for technological innovations. Plenty of geniuses have made great scientific discoveries and technological inventions without possessing extended formal education. However, with the explosion and accumulation of scientific knowledge and technological advancement over the past few centuries, the likelihood of anyone making such discoveries and inventions without extended formal training is slim to nonexistent. Nearly all professional researchers in developed countries have gone through extended formal training and qualified for advanced degrees, typically at the doctoral level. As a result, doctoral degree holders are the primary producers of scientific research papers.

In 1982, China granted its first doctoral degrees to six individuals. There were only a handful of doctoral degree programs in the country, and annual admissions of doctoral students remained under ten thousand until 1994. Fewer than forty thousand doctoral students were admitted each year until 2003. Then the number of doctoral students dramatically increased in 2004, and now China boasts the largest number of doctoral degree programs—and thus doctoral students—in the world.[11] But

China's boom in science papers and patents happened around the same time as its dramatic increase in doctoral students. It's unlikely that the newly admitted doctoral students had much to do with the miraculous growth in science papers and patent applications since they were just beginning their training in scientific research.

Of course, China does not have to rely on only doctoral graduates from its own institutions. Instead, it has taken measures to attract researchers trained in foreign countries, especially Chinese nationals who left home to study overseas. Those strategies have not been successful in attracting individuals with doctoral degrees, however. Even in 2012, the year when a record-breaking number of Chinese students with overseas educations came home, only 5.8 percent of the 160,000 returnees had doctoral degrees.[12] Although no data are available to count the exact number of foreign-trained individuals with doctoral degrees who are now working in China, the number can't be significant judging from the small percentage in 2012.

A more telling figure is the proportion of advanced-degree holders on university faculties. Universities are the primary institutions producing scientific research publications. They are also the most active recruiters of advanced-degree holders. In 2012, out of nearly 1.5 million full-time college teachers in China, fewer than 20 percent (255,799) held a doctoral degree, according to statistics from the Chinese Ministry of Education.[13] And that was a remarkable change from 1998, when only 18,921 college professors in China held a doctoral degree. In 2003, when China's research publications and patent applications began to skyrocket, only 53,612 of the 724,658 full-time teachers in China's higher education institutions held a doctoral degree.

In other words, the majority of China's science and technology workforce did not have anywhere near the level of education found in developed countries such as the United States, where a doctoral degree is a prerequisite for holding a university faculty position in virtually all institutions of higher education and typically for professional research positions as well. Yet China produced millions of research publications and patent applications. What's behind the miracle?

PUBLISH OR PERISH

The billion-dollar industry of fraudulent publication points to one of the major reasons for China's achievement: competition. The central government—the modern equivalent of the emperor—dictates career pathways for virtually all professionals, from college professors to professional researchers. There is a national career ladder that puts professionals into different ranks of positions, with corresponding salaries, social status, and other benefits. Traditionally these ranks are aligned with the ranks of government officials. For example, an associate professor is the equivalent of a deputy director in a government department. A full professor is about the same rank as a department director. Although in the United States, professionals have different ranks and fall into some sort of a salary schedule, what a particular rank signifies varies with the institution. The Chinese system, in contrast, is highly centralized, and the same criteria apply to everyone. The central government also controls the distribution of such positions in each institution, allocating a certain number of slots for each level. In other words, one institution may have many qualified candidates for promotion to the next level, but the number of positions at the next level is limited. As a result, only a certain number can advance, creating an intense mechanism for competition.

Moreover, the Chinese government dictates the criteria for career advancement. And one of its primary criteria is publication. In a fiercely competitive situation in which publication has become a professional necessity—both to keep a job and to move ahead—the motivation to publish is naturally high. China has more than 17 million K–12 teachers; 1 million college teachers; over 5 million engineers and scientists in state enterprises; 300,000 professional researchers; 700,000 scientists, engineers, and technicians in agriculture; and 3.6 million medical professionals, all of whom need to show publications in order to keep their jobs or seek promotion. Most of these individuals are not engaged in research and have not been trained to be researchers. Publication is not their passion, and it does not lie at the core of what they do. Yet if they want to survive professionally, they have to publish.

What do you do when you don't care about something but have to deal with it? Spending a few hundred dollars to buy a publication strikes many Chinese professionals as a reasonable, albeit unethical, choice. It is unlikely that a paper purchased online will qualify for important science journals, especially those published in English outside China. And papers published in fake journals are not counted as China's total paper output. However, the mechanism that drives Chinese professionals to purchase papers and false publications also fuels the production of legitimate publications. If the mechanism is powerful enough to motivate so many professionals to commit fraud, it is undoubtedly powerful enough to motivate millions of professionals to do real research and publish it. With such a large population of individuals driven to produce research papers, it should not be surprising that some of them make it into SCI-indexed journals, which vary in quality and selectivity. The 116,000 papers published by Chinese researchers in 2012 represent only a

> *The mechanism that drives Chinese professionals to purchase papers and false publications also fuels the production of legitimate publications.*

sliver (about 1 percent) of the total number of papers produced by the tens of millions of professionals required to publish each year.

IT PAYS TO PUBLISH

Sticks work; so do carrots. While many Chinese professionals are driven to produce papers in order to keep their job or seek promotion, others are driven by the prospect of extra cash or perks.

In 2009, Jinggangshan or Jinggang Mountains, the first revolutionary base established by Mao Zedong and his Communist comrades nearly a century ago, became the center of national and even international attention again, this time for trying to fulfill the wish of the Chinese government to advance science and technology. A university is now located in—and named after—the mountains. In just two years, two of Jinggangshan University's professors published seventy papers in the UK-based journal *Acta Crystallographica Section E*. Alas, these papers were retracted in 2009 because they had reported fabricated and falsified data. The journal later announced more retractions. Although the thirty or so papers retracted later were not authored by these same two professors, most of them came from researchers at the same university.

Further investigation undertaken by Chinese journalists revealed that virtually all of the seventy retracted papers were authored by one researcher, Zhong Hua, who had been recruited to the university with a master's degree in 2004. Zhong discovered a quick way to rack up international publications through *Acta Crystallographica Section E*, a legitimate open-access online journal that was once included in SCI.[14] However the journal is considered a megajournal, a crossover between a traditional scientific journal and a database. Its role is to publish reports of new crystal structures, so if a structure is new, it gets published. The journal has been a major outlet for Chinese researchers in this field. A *Nature* report published in 2010 says that "half of the 200,000-odd crystal structures published by the journal during the past five years have come from China."[15]

With forty-one papers published in the journal between 2006 and 2008, Zhong Hua had been quite successful. He was generous with that success, sharing it with his friends. One day his wife, who came from the same city as the wife of another researcher, Liu Tao, told her that Zhong Hua could help her husband get SCI publications. Liu accepted the offer, even though his research field had nothing to do with identifying crystal structures. In the end, he had twenty-nine papers published under his name but produced by Zhong.

For his forty-one papers, Zhong would have received roughly 200,000 yuan (about $30,000) in cash prizes, twice as much as the average college professor's annual salary. A 5,000 yuan cash prize was awarded to each SCI paper publication.[16]

To motivate research productivity, Chinese universities, research organizations, and governments have devised an elaborate system that gives out generous cash prizes to researchers for their publications, patents, contracts, and grants. The amount may differ across institutions, but the system follows a similar framework. Reflecting the culture's hierarchical mind-set, publications are ordered in terms of the outlet's prestige and importance. Journals and publishing houses are each graded by government agencies and accorded a particular status, which then is used to decide the size of the cash prize. For example, if Zhong had one paper published in the US-based journal *Science* or the UK-based *Nature*, the two journals considered most prestigious in China, he would have received 100,000 yuan.

The carrot approach seems to have worked well for Jinggangshan University, which was constituted as a teaching college in 2003 after combining a few vocational and technical colleges similar to community colleges in the United States. In 2007, Jinggangshan was granted university status by the Ministry of Education. It offers degrees predominantly at the undergraduate level, with only eighteen master's students in a student body of sixteen thousand. Most of its faculty members, more than one thousand, do not have the necessary training in research, nor are their primary responsibilities researching and publishing. In 2013, about 15 percent of the faculty held a doctoral degree; about one-third had only a bachelor's degree. Yet in the five years before 2003, Jinggangshan University had 4,600 research papers and 254 books published, an achievement as astonishing as the nation's.[17]

A CHINESE HEART

Another force driving China's miracle is patriotism. To inspire scientific and technological innovations, the Chinese government makes good use of the millennium-old Chinese spirit instilled in its intellectuals: love for country.

On February 26, 2003, celebrities and high-level government officials gathered in Shanghai to hear an important announcement. With much fanfare, a panel of leading computer scientists announced their unanimous approval of Hanxin #1, a computer chip invented in China. The experts believed that the chip was the first in China and cutting-edge internationally. Widely reported and celebrated, the announcement marked an important milestone in China's history of chip development.

Three years later, another announcement came. In 2006, after two months of investigation, a panel of experts commissioned by the Ministry of Education, the Ministry of Science and Technology, and the Shanghai government unanimously concluded that "in the research and development process of the Hanxin series of chips, Chen Jin has engaged in serious frauds and deception. He deceived the evaluation experts, Shanghai Jiaotong University,

R&D teams, local and the central governments, as well as the media and the public."[18]

In three years, Chen Jin had gone from national hero to con artist. Who *was* he?

Chen earned a doctoral degree in computer engineering from the University of Texas in 1997. He then worked at Motorola for about three years before joining the faculty of Shanghai Jiaotong University, one of the most prestigious engineering schools in China (and the alma mater of China's former president, Jiang Zemin). At the university, Chen was recruited to work on computer chips. In 2000, the Chinese government announced that it wanted its "research and production capacity for software to reach or approximate advanced international standards." By 2010, China was to "become one of the primary research and production bases for the microchip industry in the world."[19] The announcement came with a series of policies and grants propelling the country toward its goal: inventing its own computer technology.

Chen was given funds, personnel, and facility to create the Hanxin Lab in March 2002. The name was carefully chosen to reflect national pride and patriotism. *Han* means the Chinese people, and *xin* means chip but also has the same pronunciation as "heart" in Mandarin. Within less than a year, Chen and his small team—fewer than ten, mostly graduate students at Shanghai Jiaotong—presented the miraculous Hanxin #1, a high-end advanced digital signal processing chip that passed the inspection of leading computer experts and won national recognition. By contrast, it had taken Motorola more than three years and team of over one hundred professional engineers to develop one of its chips, the DSP56800E.

Chen's success won him considerable recognition. He was appointed dean of the College of Microelectronics at Shanghai Jiaotong University, awarded the distinguished and exclusive title of Changjiang Scholar by the Ministry of Education, and named a National Advanced Worker in Science and Technology. Between 2003 and 2005, he received government funding in excess of 100 million yuan (about $18 million) for further R&D. He continued to produce more advanced chips, from Hanxin #2 to Hanxin #5, and filed twelve patent applications for his inventions.

In January 2006, a message accusing Chen of fraud and deception was posted on an online bulletin board. Five months later, it became clear that Chen had never invented the chip. He had bought five Motorola chips and hired migrant workers to carefully replace the Motorola logo with Hanxin's. The "Chinese hearts" were nothing more than commercially available chips manufactured by Motorola.

MORE INVENTIONS THAN YOUNG EDISON

Another incentive for Chinese achievement is the lure of extra points for college admissions. Just the rumor that a national patent can boost a high school graduate's chances in the fiercely competitive college admission process was enough to generate hundreds of patents in an ordinary school in Dalian.[20]

A 2008 story in the *Bandao Chenbao* (*Peninsula Morning News*) reported that one ninth-grade class had been granted over twenty patents. Students in this Dalian school had been granted over five hundred patents in the previous three years. "Over 30% of our students have national patents," a teacher told the reporter, "but ours are not

"Over 30% of our students have national patents," a teacher told the reporter, "but ours are not the highest. Of all middle schools in Dalian, our school is only slightly above average."

the highest. Of all middle schools in Dalian, our school is only slightly above average in terms of percentage of students owning national patents."

The phenomenon stretches nationwide. A secondary school in Wuhan collected more than two thousand patents in about eight years. One of its students was granted twelve patents in a single year. The total number of patents granted to elementary and secondary school students increased from two in 2002 to nearly six thousand in 2011, a five-hundred-fold jump in less than ten years. In the seventeen years before 2002, only thirty patents total had been filed by students K–12.[21]

In students, patent fever is largely driven by real or rumored policies that patents can add extra points to the college admission exam (*gaokao*). China has decentralized admissions decisions about bonus points based on ethnicity, special talents, and other achievements, allowing provincial government officials and some selected universities to make the judgment calls. Although there is no uniform policy across the nation about whether—or to what degree—a patent can be counted toward college admission scores, which are typically based on *gaokao*, there is widespread belief that patents can help dramatically. And that belief is deliberately perpetuated by businesses that, for a fee, help students file patent applications.

Inventions certainly helped Yingying Wu, a controversial student at Beijing Normal University. In December 2006, the university held a press conference about her accomplishments. In this highly unusual event, reporters were told that Wu, a twenty-one-year-old senior studying psychology, had made one hundred inventions, held three patents, had been appointed chair member of the Association of Machinery Computing, and had been hired as vice president of Topcoder, an American company that organizes computer programming contests. Wu's inventions and patents had been a critical factor in her admission to the university three years earlier since her *gaokao* scores were below the university's cutoff score. Her story had already been sent to many media outlets; this particular press conference was to announce her candidacy for China's national Student of the Year Award.[22]

As soon as her story was told, Wu became the hottest college student in China. But the initial admiration and praise were quickly replaced by a flurry of online postings and media reports casting doubt on her accomplishments.[23] The truth is that her accomplishments were grossly exaggerated. Yes, Topcoder had made her vice president for Asia, but she was the only employee in the Asian office, and Topcoder was a much smaller company than the media were led to believe. She was not a chair member of ACM but an assistant to the one of its committees. She held not three patents but two. There was no evidence of her one hundred inventions, a total that would have outstripped Thomas Edison at the same age. After initially refusing to respond to media inquiries about the accuracy of Wu's story, officials at Beijing Normal University admitted that there were some inaccuracies and exaggeration in Wu's résumé.[24] Her stardom ended soon after it began.

LITTLE CLEVERNESS AND JUNK PAPERS

Wu and other young inventers have contributed significantly to the total number of China's patents. However, a large proportion of China's patents have been called "junk patents" or, at best, *xiao congming* (small cleverness). "The corporate and academic opinion is that 'over 50% or even 80% of Chinese patents are junk,'" notes a reporter at *China IP*

A large proportion of China's patents have been called "junk patents" or, at best, xiao congming (small cleverness).

Magazine.[25] One of Wu's patents, for instance, was called Rapid Search Method and Its Dictionary, which according to the abstract was "a method to quickly find a word in a dictionary through the index attached at the side of the dictionary. The index indicates the location in the dictionary of the first and second syllable of a word."[26] This was essentially the same method that the *American Heritage Dictionary* series was already using.

Wu's patents belonged to the "utility model" category, which most developed countries do not consider true inventions. Granted, she filed her first patent application at the age of fifteen, an impressive accomplishment for a teenager. But while such patents might prove useful, they are unlikely to be commercialized and bring significant value to the economy. They're not likely to help realize China's dream for true scientific and technological innovations.

Patents like Wu's make up the majority of China's patents. China grants three types of patents: invention, utility model, and design. Invention patents can be granted to both products and processes and must meet standards of novelty, inventiveness, and practical use, determined by a review process called substantive examination. In contrast, utility model patents are granted without review because the expectation of "inventiveness" is far lower. Design patents, like utility model patents, improve products' appearance and are granted without the substantive examination review. Both utility model and design patents are far easier to obtain and far less innovative than invention patents, and they are generally considered to be of lower quality. In many developed countries, invention patents are the only ones granted.

In 2011, out of the 1.5 million patent applications received by the State Intellectual Property Office in China from both domestic and foreign entities in 2011, just about one-third were invention patents. More, 36 percent, were utility model patent applications. Most of the utility applications came from Chinese entities, which filed 1.5 million patent applications all told. Only 28 percent of that total were invention patents; 38 percent were utility model patents. In comparison, 86 percent of patent applications from foreign entities were invention patents, and only 3 percent were utility model patents.

In 2012, the number of patent applications had another significant increase, but the proportion of invention patents remained low. In more than 2 million applications, the percentage of invention patents remained about one-third. The percentage was much lower in the number of patents actually granted—about 217,000 out of 1,255,000, so about 18 percent.[27]

The dubious quality of patents in China has been openly acknowledged and widely discussed by Chinese officials. "Our nation's patent quality remains at a relatively low level," said Tian Lipu, director of China's State Office of Intellectual Property, at a press conference in 2013. "Unlike the cutting-edge and innovative high-tech patents, a lot more of our patents are improvement inventions, lower quality utility model and design patents."[28] A comprehensive study of China's patent quality, released in 2012 by the European Union Chamber of Commerce, concluded, "Analysis of a variety of patent statistics suggests that China's progress in patent quality lags behind its rates of patent filings," as indicated by a broad range of measures:

> There are higher ratios of domestic to foreign filings of invention patents in EU countries sampled than in China. There are significantly lower average life-spans of Chinese patents and lower percentages of patents in-force owned by domestic filers vs. foreign filers in China compared with the rates in EU and other countries sampled; higher rates of utility model invalidations than invention patent and design patent invalidations; concerning rates of patents filed solely for malicious prosecution actions, which may be made up more so of utility models than other types of patents; poor scores in terms of patent citations; and empirical econometric analyses

generally show foreign enterprises at large do not typically file
patents on breakthrough inventions in China. China also has
lacklustre scores on several other patent quality indicators.[29]

China's research publications have the same problem, when
tested for quality. *Nature* reported that a 2010 survey commissioned by the Chinese Ministry of Science found that "roughly
one-third of more than 6,000 surveyed across six top institutions
admitted to plagiarism, falsification or fabrication."[30] In 2008,
Helen Zhang, editor of the prestigious *Journal of Zhejiang University-
Science*, pioneered the use of software to spot plagiarism in submis-
sions. "In almost two years, we find about 31 percent of papers
with unreasonable copy[ing] and plagiarism," she told NPR in
2011.[31] In another astonishing case, a medical research paper
published in 1997 was found to have been plagiarized six times
by twenty-five coauthors at sixteen institutions in 2010.[32] Despite
significant advances in medical technology, the plagiarists
continued to report similar results using virtually identical
language.

Fraud aside, the overall lower quality of China's research
papers is also indicated by another figure: the average number of
times a paper has been referenced by other papers. Although the
overall number of citations of Chinese papers has increased significantly, the average remains much lower than the world's
average: 6.92 times compared to 10.69 times.[33]

In short, the quantity of China's scientific and technological
output looks more than impressive, but the quality of its patents
and research publications is abysmal. China still trails many developed countries when it comes to real innovation and significant
patents. In other words, while the grand wish of the government
has been realized in terms of quantity, the government has not
gotten what it really wants. The trillions of dollars China has spent
on its scientific and technological Great Leap Forward has had

an outcome almost identical to the previous Great Leap: lots of steel without much value and rampant cheating.

BY DESIGN

The high percentage of low-quality products and fraudulent research seriously hampers China's ambition for indigenous innovations. Unless it can reverse the trend, China is likely to produce even more low-quality inventions, and cheating is unlikely to stop. The government has repeatedly called for higher ethical standards, handed down

Any criticism of this authoritarian culture is viewed as un-Chinese and anti-Chinese, inviting not rational discussion but emotional attacks.

severe punishment to violators, and tweaked policies. But the problem runs deeper, and it's almost unsolvable. It is rooted in an authoritarian culture that has continued for thousands of years, and very few Chinese, particularly those in leadership, have any desire to change that culture. In fact, any criticism of this authoritarian culture is viewed as un-Chinese and anti-Chinese, inviting not rational discussion but emotional attacks and quite possibly political and legal troubles.

The current approach to scientific and technological innovation is in design no different from the approach that built the Great Wall. The emperors had their wishes realized at great cost, without necessarily reaping the intended benefits. The same approach produced a stunning number of medals for China in the Olympic Games. The methodology is not unique to China; its fundamental characteristics are shared by all authoritarian cultures. This approach is highly effective in accomplishing pre-determined goals and thus often wins praise. But what makes the approach effective is also what makes it ineffective—and at times disastrous.

Reason 1: Wishful Thinking

The authoritarian approach typically starts with a grand vision conceived by the central, most powerful, dominating entity—which can be an individual, such as an emperor, or a group of individuals, such as a corporate board or the politburo of the Communist Party government. Having a grand vision is not a problem in itself, but often the grand vision in a dictatorial system lacks sufficient information about reality. In a system that demands compliance, it's hard for different and opposing views to reach the authority. And when they do, it's easy for the dictator to ignore them. As a result, the vision may be completely impossible. Numerous emperors in ancient China, for example, spent vast sums and put countless alchemists to death, all in a vain effort to realize the vision of developing medicine for eternal life.

China's vision for instant, breakthrough innovations is an example of such wishful thinking. The desire is understandable and easy to appreciate, but it ignores a number of basic realities. First, modern science and technological innovations require specialized knowledge of the existing literature, which has accumulated over a long period of time. Innovations cannot be made without individuals who have studied this literature and acquired the necessary know-how. Moreover, breakthrough innovations cannot be made by one or two great individuals. Breakthroughs require a community of experts. China did not and still does not have enough well-trained individuals to produce the quantity of scientific and technological innovations the government has demanded by 2015.

Second, modern scientific and technological innovations also require hardware, knowledge of the processes of management and support, and established communities with platforms and opportunities for peer interactions. China has invested large amounts of money to acquire hardware, build labs, and purchase equipment, but except in a few universities and national laboratories, China's research facilities are still not well enough equipped to generate the desired outcomes. It also takes time to learn how to manage and support scientific research and establish the norms and practices of scientific communities.

Third, diligence is necessary for innovations, but diligence alone is insufficient. True creative work also requires inspiration, talent, and passion. One can be forced to memorize Shakespeare, but one cannot be forced to produce plays of Shakespearean quality. Simply mandating people to come up with great innovations in a preset time frame does not necessarily mean they can and will do so. For that reason, although milestones and objectives are important, it is unrealistic to set specific time lines and targets for innovations.

In sum, China's grand vision for innovation was admirable but unrealistic. Yet the government pressed forward. Using both stick and carrot, China's central government mobilized institutions and professionals to deliver the dream in spite of the unfavorable realities.

Reason 2: Upward Accountability

What makes China so effective at executing the wishes of the central government is its system's upward accountability. An essential characteristic of a hierarchically organized society is upward accountability, in which lower-level government officials serve at the pleasure of higher-level officials. While career ladders exist in all societies and organizations, in a centrally governed society there is only one career ladder that all must climb. That means the only hope for upward mobility is to be chosen by the upper-level authority. As a result, government officials hoping to be promoted work very hard to please their superiors. As long as the superiors are happy, the promotion is almost certain, regardless of how a given official is viewed by peers or subordinates. Moreover, the Confucian tradition of piety and loyalty deeply rooted in the Chinese culture dictates absolute obedience to authority, be it the emperor, father, or a higher-ranked official.

Upward accountability makes it extremely easy to execute the will of the central authority. As soon as the central authority expresses a desire, no matter how unrealistic, lower-level officials adopt it as an order and pass it on to their subordinates. Few dare question the order, for that might displease their superiors. In addition, each time a new wish is issued, new opportunities arise for some officials to demonstrate their ability to deliver the wish better than their peers and thus earn recognition or promotion. Even those who aren't angling for a promotion have to implement the orders just to keep their current position and win precious resources that are centrally controlled.

Upward accountability not only incentivizes officials to show off how well they can fulfill their superior's wish, but also protects, even encourages, cheating. In the controversy of Yingying Wu, the motivation of Beijing Normal University was called into question. Beijing Normal University was compared to the 1950s communes that raced to exaggerate their productivity during the first disastrous Great Leap Forward. Some suggested that the university was working with the Chinese Communist Ministry of Propaganda to create a new model of Chinese college student in order to fulfill the government's wish for innovation. The university denied the accusation, but admitted that the intention of Beijing Normal University was to promote Wu as an intellectual star, a model of the "creative and innovative students" that China needed, according to an official of the university's Propaganda Department.[34] The deputy party secretary of Beijing Normal University, Zheng E, was "pleased that the University was able to cultivate students like Wu"; at the press conference, she shared the university's experiences in fostering creative and innovative talent. In other words, Beijing Normal University wanted to promote itself as an institution that cultivates the talents the government desires.

In China's campaign for greater innovation, as soon as the central government issued state plans and targets, provincial governments created policies and measures to motivate their local governments and institutions. Nearly all layers of government and all institutions developed similar plans and targets.[35] Every university and research entity now has policies that mandate and incentivize their employees to produce patents and research papers. The outcome, not surprisingly, is a nationwide race to out-innovate each other.

Reason 3: A Uniform and Quantifiable Standard

In order to reduce variations and avoid corruption, the centralized approach requires a uniform, quantifiable, easily measured standard. Since the authority controls all resources, including financial and other possible benefits such as promotion, housing, residence rights, college admissions, and honors, it needs a way to objectively and fairly award these resources. In a large society with a long history of *guanxi*, or relationships, the best way to do that is to quantify just how much organizations, local governments, and individuals contribute to the wish of the higher authority. Those quantities are then translated into quotas for institutions, made part of individuals' responsibilities, and used to award punishment and prizes accordingly.

In the first Great Leap Forward, the measure was the amount of steel and grain produced. In the campaign for innovation, it is the number of patent applications and publications.

China has therefore developed an elaborate and uniform mechanism to determine the contribution of researchers. It has officially published guidelines for ranking the quality of patents and papers based on their outlets. Patents registered in patent offices outside China are worth a lot more than those registered in the Chinese State Intellectual Property Office. The same is true

The rigid scheme China uses to evaluate innovations also reflects the Chinese tradition of believing in established authority—which in itself can hinder innovation.

for publications and conference presentations. Although many institutions outside China, in developed countries, have similar practices in evaluating the contribution of researchers, their rules are not nearly as steadfast and rigid. Other systems leave room for discretion because different fields may have different practices and because true innovations may not be recognized (and may even be rejected) by the authorities that control existing outlets for publication and conference presentations. The rigid scheme China uses to evaluate innovations by the recognition they receive from established authorities also reflects the Chinese tradition of believing in established authority—which in itself can hinder innovation.

Furthermore, because quantity matters more than quality, Chinese researchers learn to game the system by producing large quantities of low-quality products—easily had patents, like the utility model patents; insignificant papers; plagiarized patents and papers; and patents and papers purchased outright. The motivation is not to create breakthrough innovations but to meet the needs of the authority and reap the due reward. For example, a group of Chinese researchers found that the most influential factor determining the quality of China's patents is motivation. There are different types of motivation at play, but the primary motivations are all utilitarian. "Seeking promotion and prizes" was the most frequent reason given for patent application. The second most frequent reason was "to meet the mandate of the authority," followed by "being recognized as a high-tech enterprise and receiving tax benefits."[36]

THE EMPEROR IS FOOLED

By nature, Chinese are no less creative than other people, nor are they less inclined to take risks or more predisposed to cheating. But in a system that imposes unrealistic expectations through carefully orchestrated mechanisms of punishment and reward—with the results decided by meticulously designed and seemingly objective measures—individuals have to develop certain skills and strategies to survive and prosper. China's rampant cheating and high percentage of low-quality patents and papers are the consequence of those survival skills and strategies.

Cheating is risky given the consequences. It's even riskier than proposing an innovative idea. But when one is unable to produce the mandated "innovations" in time, cheating begins to look like the only choice. Judging from the many cases of cheating and various other strategies to satisfy the authorities, the Chinese students and researchers have been highly creative. But they've used their creativity to find practical ways to satisfy the authority, not to improve scientific and tech-

> *When one is unable to produce the mandated "innovations" in time, cheating begins to look like the only choice.*

nological research and development. The "small cleverness" that can be observed in the low-quality patents, various forms of plagiarism, and canny methods of avoiding detection is certainly a form of creativity, just as running a fake publishing house requires a certain entrepreneurship. But all of this creativity and entrepreneurship is misdirected because of the unrealistic wishes of authority: produce innovations in specified areas, following the required formats, verified by established authorities, and within a specific time frame.

In summary, the fundamental reason behind China's inability to produce breakthrough innovations is the cultural mind-set that innovation can be mandated by pressure from above and achieved by effort alone. In other words, if there is a wish, a system to impose the wish on individuals, and a way to verify the efforts of individuals, innovation can be achieved. But that mind-set violates the basic logic of creativity. Innovation comes from the work of free-spirited people driven by passion, equipped with the necessary expertise and resources, and granted the autonomy to explore. And free-spirited people are what China lacks and actively discourages through its educational system—the issue we deal with in the rest of this book.

6

HELL TO HEAVEN

The Making of the World's Best
and Worst Education

"No one, after 12 years of Chinese education, has any chance to receive a Nobel prize, even if he or she goes to Harvard, Yale, Oxford, or Cambridge for college," blogged Zheng Yefu, a professor at China's Peking University and author of *The Pathology of Chinese Education*, a popular Chinese book published in 2013.[1] "Out of the one billion people who have been educated in Mainland China since 1949, there has been no Nobel prize winner," Zheng wrote in an article. "This forcefully testifies [to] the power of education in destroying creativity on behalf of the [Chinese] society."[2]

Zheng was talking about the same education that made China the envy of the world. Just a few months after Zheng's comments, results of the 2012 Programme for International Student Assessment (PISA) were released. For the second time in a row, Shanghai, the most developed and cosmopolitan city in China, led the world in math, reading, and science. It was not the only Chinese entity that earned outstanding PISA scores. Although their data were not included in the official PISA report, students in Zhejiang Province, most of them from rural schools, performed almost as well.[3] They topped the scores of every other educational system except Shanghai's.

The PISA scores don't necessarily disprove Zheng's point, because test scores are not the same as creativity, and Chinese students have been known for being great test takers at the cost

> *Test scores are not the same as creativity, and Chinese students have been known for being great test takers at the cost of creativity.*

of creativity. However, Andreas Schleicher, the de facto spokesperson for PISA, has been trying. He points out that a lot more of "Shanghai's 15-year-olds can conceptualize, generalize, and creatively use information" than can American or European students.[4] In Shanghai, more than 30 percent of the students demonstrated such abilities through the PISA, Schleicher says, compared to only 2 percent in America and 3 percent in Europe.[5] He insists that students in Shanghai were not simply good at taking tests: "The biggest surprise from Shanghai to the world was not that students did well on reproducing subject matter content but that they were very very good in those higher order skills."[6]

Armed with PISA scores, Schleicher has helped create another wave of Sinophilism some four hundred years after the Jesuit missionaries. However, just like the Jesuit missionaries and their fellow European Sinophiles who were fooled by shallow observations, Schleicher was deceived by his PISA, which, regardless of the claims of the Organization for Economic Cooperation and Development (OECD), is still a test: it measures students' ability to come up with answers deemed correct by the authority. Moreover, PISA is confined to three subjects. There is far more to life's success than what can be measured by standardized tests in three subjects. Even Schleicher concedes that "the kind of things that are easy to test in an exam like this are becoming less relevant."[7]

Yet he and his fellow Sinophiles are not entirely wrong in pronouncing China's—or at least Shanghai's—the best education system in the world. Chinese students have consistently been top performers on international assessments, have collected a remarkable number of prizes and awards in international academic contests such as the science and math Olympiads, and have demonstrated academic excellence in many other ways."[8] But the Sinophiles forget that China also has the world's worst education system in terms of its capacity for cultivating creative inventors, innovators, and entrepreneurs. It has not produced Nobel winners in science, transformative technological inventions, or groundbreaking scientific discoveries in proportion to its population. The majority of its patents and scientific papers, despite their impressive quantity, are of relative low quality, as we discussed in the previous chapter.

Worse yet, the Sinophiles fail to realize that what makes the Chinese education the best is precisely what makes it the worst. In their efforts to propagate the secrets that brought China its great PISA performance, they don't talk about the downside of Chinese education or "the costs of Shanghai's education success story" that have been pointed out by Jiang Xueqin, deputy principal of Tsinghua University High School, and many others, including the Chinese government.[9]

The most damaging aspect of Chinese education is its effectiveness in eliminating individual differences, suppressing intrinsic motivation, and imposing conformity. The Chinese education system is a well-designed and continuously perfected machine that effectively and efficiently transmits a narrow band of

The Chinese education system is a well-designed and continuously perfected machine that effectively and efficiently transmits a narrow band of predetermined content and cultivates prescribed skills.

predetermined content and cultivates prescribed skills. Moreover, the system determines people's livelihood. Because it is the only path to social mobility, people follow it eagerly. As a result, it produces great performances in areas the authority determines to be worthy—and PISA happens to test skills and content in precisely those areas. Unless and until the system changes, Chinese students will continue to top the PISA rankings—and China will continue to lack the pool of diverse and innovative talents it needs. Thus we have this paradox: while many Western observers such as Andreas Schleicher envy China's PISA performance, the Chinese are working hard to dismantle the factors responsible for that success.[10]

The cultural legacy that has shaped China's educational system is reflected in the saying, "All life's pursuits are worth less than [the] scholarly quest." In China, there has been only one heaven on earth: a socially recognized profession that brings honor, fame, and respect.

ONE HEAVEN

"I have disgraced, dishonored my alma mater," Lu Buxuan said, his voice choked, in a public lecture at Peking University in 2013.[11] A graduate of the university, Lu had become a well-known and controversial figure a decade earlier when he was discovered working as a butcher in Xi'an. In 1985, he was admitted to Peking University as the highest-scoring student in his county. He was assigned a post after graduation, as it was the policy that all college graduates were assigned a job by the government. But in 1999, he was not earning enough in his post so he decided to open a butcher shop. To reflect his scholarly background, he named the shop *Yanjing Roudian*—The Butcher with Glasses.

Lu's story caused a national uproar in China. Opinions varied, but most felt butchery was not a decent profession for a graduate of the most prestigious university in China. People roundly criticized the government for not having taken care of its well-educated scholar. A few months after the story broke in the national media, the local government gave Lu a job as an editor in the Archives Department. "We had talked with him way before his story was reported in the media," said a local government official in self-defense. "In 2001, we offered him several positions, but it did not work out. Last year when the media were all over his story, we offered him several positions again...Considering his interest and strength, we think he should work in the Archives Department."[12]

Lu turned his shop over to his wife and began to work for the government, but a few years later, he returned to the shop. He met another graduate-turned-butcher from Peking University in 2008 and teamed up with him. Now he has written a book, *The Study of Pork Marketing*, and opened a butchery school. He and his fellow graduate have also started a large chain of meat stores. They were honored with an invitation to speak at their alma mater in April 2013, when China's 7 million college graduates faced the toughest year for finding jobs.[13] Yet despite his apparent success, Lu still thought himself a failure and a disgrace. "I am the textbook of what not to become," he told his audience.

Lu's story exemplifies the first factor that contributes to both China's educational success and its failure: the cultural values that narrowly define worthwhile accomplishment. For thousands of years, government positions have been sold as the only respectable job in China. Ranked by status, the professions proceed downward from *shi* (government officials) to *nong* (farmers), *gong* (craftsman), and *shang* (merchants). Confucius said that "the student, having completed his learning, should apply himself to be a government officer."[14] With social status come material rewards: political power, job security, handsome income, housing, and other fringe benefits. Even today in a drastically transformed and far more diverse China, the most prized jobs remain government positions. In 2013, about 1.5 million people competed for approximately 20,000 government positions in the Chinese national civil servant exam.[15]

The fact that Lu has not achieved a high-level government job or a scholarly position that puts his literary skills to good use is a disgrace not only to him but also to his alma mater. Lu is a victim of traditional Chinese education, blogged Shi Yuzhi, a professor at Singapore National University and author of *Why Cannot China Have Grand Masters*.[16] "Lu Buxuan has surrendered to the traditional value of Chinese education...According to the Chinese value system, selling pork is a job for the illiterate," not the educated. Conversely, the purpose of education is to obtain a government position or another highly ranked job that hovers well above the struggle for daily necessities.

This narrow definition of accomplishment is a powerful way to homogenize individuals by discouraging any pursuit that does not serve the emperor or government. This is one of the reasons China didn't have the industrialists, naturalists, technologists, inventors, and entrepreneurs it needed to start an industrial revolution. These professions were all considered disgraceful compared to the scholar-official. Education, in the traditional Chinese perspective, should not be applied to help cultivate these less honorable professions. Education in China is, in essence, a process through which those willing to comply are homogenized and those unwilling or unable to comply—but quite

> *Education in China is, in essence, a process through which those willing to comply are homogenized, and those unwilling or unable to comply—but quite possibly talented or interested in other, nonscholarly pursuits— are eliminated.*

possibly talented or interested in other, nonscholarly pursuits—
are eliminated.

This narrow definition of success also undergirds the widespread belief that Chinese culture places a high value on education. "For centuries, Chinese people have believed in the value of
education for the nation's well-being as well as for their own personal advancement," wrote the late Harold Stevenson and his
team of researchers at the University of Michigan twenty years
ago.[17] "China has a long tradition of valuing education highly,"
notes a document from the OECD that explains China's top performance on the PISA.[18] *New York Times* columnist Nicholas Kristof
maintains that "the greatest strength of the Chinese system is the
Confucian reverence for education that is steeped into the
culture."[19] "Mr. Schleicher says the [PISA] results reveal a picture
of a society investing individually and collectively in education,"
a BBC reporter wrote after interviewing Andreas Schleicher in
2012.[20]

The Chinese do indeed value education, but out of necessity,
not out of choice. Valuing education is simply a survival strategy.
It evolved to cope with an authoritarian system that had instilled
a very narrow definition of success: there is only one heaven, and
education is the only way to get there.

ONE SMALL HEAVEN

The number of socially respected professions and positions in
China is small, making the heaven a tiny place that millions of
young people have no way of reaching. The few who do then
climb mountains carved from another Chinese value: hierarchy.
As a historically authoritarian society organized around the
Confucian philosophy, China gives a hierarchical order to every
facet of life. Value is always positional, established by comparison
to other persons, places, or things. Moreover, there are socially
recognized and sometimes government-imposed criteria to judge

relative value. For example, China's national leaders sit atop a multilayered pyramid in which the premier is above the vice premiers, who are above ministers and provincial governors, who are above vice ministers and deputy governors, who are above director-generals of *ting* or *ju* (departments), who are above their deputies, who are above the leaders of a county, then villages and townships. This hierarchy is used to distribute everything from power, authority, and compensation to the location of one's seat at a dinner table. Thus, it is not enough simply to enter the right profession; one must then climb to the top in order to show accomplishment. There is no intrinsically valuable position, because there is always the next level to reach—hence the popular saying, "There is no best, only better." Being good means being better than others.

The concept of hierarchy and ranking is so solid in China that whenever a choice needs to be made about anything, the Chinese people want to know if it is top-ranked. This applies to fashion brands, restaurants, tourist spots, and of course educational institutions. When they decide which college to attend, domestic or overseas, Chinese parents and students are much more concerned about the ranking of the institution than what it actually offers or whether it suits them.

One consequence of this hierarchical view is that China will never have enough good universities, no matter how many new universities it adds or how hard it tries to improve equity. For example, the number of higher education institutions grew from 598 in 1978 to over 2,100 in 2012. The annual intake of college students increased from a mere 400,000 in 1978 to nearly 7 million in 2012. As a result, the rate of college admissions jumped from around 6 percent to almost 70 percent. Yet the competition for college has only become fiercer because it is not good enough to attend just any college. Rather, one must attend a famous college. Those who graduate from famous colleges are more respected and are given entirely different treatment in society. For instance, it has become common practice for employers, even state enterprises and governments, to openly deny and exclude job applicants based entirely on their alma mater. Job advertisements explicitly list a bachelor's degree from non-985 and non-211 universities—a small group of universities designated by the central government—as a basic qualification.[21] This open discrimination is worse than saying only a Harvard or Yale graduate can be considered for a job in the United States, since the government controls the designation. This kind of discrimination has become so rampant and caused such social dissatisfaction that the Chinese Ministry of Education had to issue an executive order forbidding it.[22] However, that order has had little effect.

Many traditional practices flow from China's hierarchical model, including the educational system's reliance on ranking. Schools are ranked by governments, then given resources according to their status. When people protested the inequity, officials stopped designating key schools and changed the category to "demonstration schools," but the change was of no practical consequence. People know the schools are still ranked at the national, provincial, and municipal levels. Students in "good" primary schools still have a better chance of entering a stronger middle school and then an even stronger high school, then moving onward to one of the 985 or 211 universities.

Classes are ranked as well. While different names are used to disguise the differences, classes are ranked from slow to fast with such euphemisms as "rocket class," "extraordinary class," and "experimental class." Often the inferior classes are simply called "slow class" or "poor student class."

Students are tested regularly and frequently: every term, every month, and in some cases every week. They are then ranked based on their test scores, and their rank is publicized. These everyday rankings have significant consequences. It is widely known that students are sorted into different classes and schools based on their rankings, but it is less well known that such sorting can happen on a monthly or even weekly basis, and the consequences can be devastating for those with lower scores. Qiangqiang, a fourteen-year-old student in a school in Hohhot, committed suicide for fear of being moved out of the "rocket class" (the fast track) because his ranking had slipped from 290 to about 600 in the class.[23]

Other hierarchical practices may not be as tragic but still do serious damage. For example, teachers commonly assign classroom seats based on student test scores. The highest scorer gets to choose his or her seat first, and the last one takes whatever seat remains at the end.[24] One school was reported to provide top-ranked students with free extra lessons, while lower-ranked students had to pay.[25] In other places, lower-ranked students had to wear green scarves in contrast to the high scorers' red scarves or were asked to take tests outside the classroom.[26]

Making education the only way to heaven lures all Chinese into the race, and the hierarchical system and constant ranking provide sustained and strong motivation for students to show that they are conforming all the time. It's no wonder Chinese students are the most hard-working bunch in the world. On average, students in Shanghai spent twice as much time on homework as the OECD average (13.7 versus 7 hours) and two and a half times the OECD average in academic studies outside school (17 versus 7.8 hours). "Time plus sweat" is the sensible explanation for Shanghai's PISA performance given by Yang Dongping, professor at Beijing University of Science

> *Outside observers praise the hard-working Chinese students, but those students, their parents, and their government have all been cursing the academic workload for decades.*

and Technology and a popular commentator on education in China.[27]

Outside observers praise the hard-working Chinese students, but those students, their parents, and their government have all been cursing the academic workload for decades. Since the 1950s, the government has been working to reduce students' academic load and pressure. As recently as 2013, the Ministry of Education issued another stern order to all schools to limit the frequency of testing and the amount of homework.[28]

Furthermore, the fierce competition for the culturally manufactured scarcity of spots in top classes, schools, and universities creates motivation for parents, teachers, and schools to do whatever they can to earn a spot in those top classes and schools, thus causing massive inequality. In a CNN commentary, Jiang Xueqin, deputy principal of Tshinhua High School, wrote about Shanghai's PISA performance: "The dog-eat-dog and winner-take-all mentality of China's school system isn't just making children unhappy and unhealthy—it's also causing cheating and bribery, leading to an unfair and unequal school system." He pointed out that wealthy families can pay or bribe to get the best teachers, extra lessons, and the best schools, thus securing a better chance for their child for a better university: "The bribery is on top of every other advantage that Shanghai's wealthy parents have bestowed upon their only child: weekend piano, math, and English classes, private tutoring, summer camp in America, vacations in Europe and above all a born-to-succeed attitude."[29]

More important, Chinese students are motivated or pressured to learn all the time, which means they learn more, but what they learn and how they learn is troublesome. "Critics see young people as learning by being fed knowledge in imposed structures, seldom left on their own to learn in their own way," writes Kai-ming Cheng, professor at the University of Hong Kong, in *Surpassing Shanghai: An Agenda for American Education Built on the World's*

Leading Systems. "They have little direct encounter with nature, for example, and little experience with the society in general. While they have developed the skills, they may not have learned how to learn."[30]

In China, the incentives for learning are all external and based on performance demonstrated by test scores. The goal is simply to be better than others in the prescribed tasks. The consequences may be high aggregated test scores in math, science, and reading. But students forgo opportunities to genuinely learn arts, music, and humanities, which the PISA does not assess. Moreover, "incentives do not just make students stressed, lonely, and unhappy—they also kill students' innate curiosity, creativity, and love of learning," writes Jiang Xueqin.[31]

ONE GATEKEEPER TO THE ONE SMALL HEAVEN

The power of the Chinese educational system to homogenize thinking is strengthened by the government's monopoly on curriculum and assessment. The Communist government has complete control over what schools teach. It also sets the criteria and the process that universities use to admit students. Even privately funded schools and universities must follow the national curriculum and use the prescribed admissions standards and process. Chinese citizens are not allowed to attend international schools that follow a non-Chinese curriculum. In fact, even if the government did not dictate the school curriculum, it would still control what schools teach and students learn as long as it controlled the selection criteria and process. The Chinese government controls education just as tightly as the emperors did in ancient times. The government is the only gatekeeper to the small heaven everyone wants to enter.

PISA lovers glorify this arrangement. In *Surpassing Shanghai*, Marc Tucker explains what high-performing countries do and

America does not do: "Virtually all high performing countries have a system of gateways marking the key transition point from basic education to job training to the work force…The national examinations at the end of the upper-secondary school are generally—but not always—the same examinations that universities in that country use for admissions," which is certainly the case in China. The advantages of such a system, Tucker notes, are numerous:

> In countries with gateway exam systems of this sort, every student has a very strong incentive to take tough courses and to work hard in school. A student who does not do that will not earn the credentials needed to achieve her dream, whether that dream is becoming a brain surgeon or an auto mechanic. Because the exams are scored externally, the student knows that the only way to move on is to meet the standard. Because they are national or provincial standards, the exams cannot be gamed. Because the exams are of a very high quality, they cannot be "test prepped"; the only way to succeed on them is to actually master the material. And because the right parties were involved in creating the exams, students know that the credentials they earn will be honored; when their high school say they are "college and career ready," colleges and employees will agree.[32]

But Tucker is wrong on all counts, at least in the case of China. Students may work hard, but they do not necessarily take tough courses. Rather, they take courses that prepare them for the exams or courses that matter only for the exams. Students do not move on to meet a high standard but to prepare for the exams. The exams can be gamed, and have often been. Teachers guess possible items, companies sell answers and wireless cheating devices to students, and students engage in all sorts of elaborate cheating.[33] In 2013, a riot broke out because a group of students in Hubei Province were stopped from executing the cheating scheme their parents purchased to ease their college entrance exam. "An angry mob of more than 2,000 people had gathered to vent its rage, smashing cars and chanting: 'We want fairness. There is no fairness if you do not let us cheat,' " read the story in the UK-based newspaper *Telegraph*.[34]

Tucker's assertion that "because the exams are of very high quality, they cannot be 'test prepped,'" is completely untrue. Chinese schools exist for test prep. Every class, every teacher, every school is about preparing for the exams. In most schools, the last year of high school is reserved exclusively for test preparation. No new content is taught. All students do the entire year is take practice tests and learn test-taking skills. Good schools often help the students exhaust all possible ways specific content might show up in an exam. Schools that have earned a reputation for preparing students for college exams have published their practice test papers and made a fortune. A large proportion of publications for children in China are practice test papers.

> *Chinese schools exist for test prep. Every class, every teacher, every school is about preparing for the exams.*

Even if Tucker were right, the system he glorifies hinders the development of creative and entrepreneurial talents in a number of ways. First, national standards and national curriculum, enforced by high-stakes testing, can at best teach students what is prescribed by the curriculum and expected by the standards. This system fails to expose students to content and skills in other areas. As a result, students talented in other areas never have the opportunity to discover those talents. Students with broader interests are discouraged, not rewarded. The system results in a population with similar skills in a narrow spectrum of talents. But especially in today's society, innovation and creativity are needed in many areas, some as yet undiscovered. Innovation and creativity come from cross-fertilization across different disciplines. A narrow educational experience hardly provides children opportunities to examine an issue from multiple disciplines.

Second, examinations such as the PISA assess cognitive skills. But creativity and entrepreneurship have a lot more to do with noncognitive skills.[35] Confidence, resilience, grit, mind-set, personality traits, social skills, and motivation have been found to be at least as important as cognitive skills in the workplace.[36] The Chinese educational system motivates students to spend all their time preparing for the examinations and gives them almost no time to cultivate noncognitive skills and traits. Meanwhile, the constant ranking and sorting put students in stressful situations that make them less confident.

Third, examinations reward the ability to find the correct answers and give those answers in expected ways. To obtain high scores, students need to learn to guess what the examiner wants and provide answers that will please the examiner. This finding and delivering of predetermined answers is antithetical to creativity, which requires the ability to come up with new solutions and pose questions that have never been asked before.

Chinese students are extremely good at well-defined problems. That is, as long as they know what they need to do to meet the expectations and have examples to follow, they do well. But in less defined situations, without routines and formulas to fall back on, they have great difficulty. In other words, they are good at solving existing problems

The system results in a population with similar skills in a narrow spectrum of talents. But especially in today's society, innovation and creativity are needed.

in predictable ways, but not at coming up with radical new solutions or inventing new problems to solve.

Fourth, a gateway system such as China's educational system replaces students' intrinsic motivation with extrinsic, utilitarian motivation. Instead of caring about what they can learn, they care about what they can get by demonstrating to the authority that they have learned what the authority wants them to learn. Getting the credential is more important than actually learning, which explains why cheating on exams is rampant. Moreover, it is possible to impose basic skills and knowledge on students without their being the least bit interested in or passionate about the subject. Thus, the Chinese system can successfully impose on students the skills and knowledge necessary for performing well on tests such as the PISA, which measures skills and content at the basic level. But no one can force those students to be creative or seek greatness if they have neither the interest nor the passion to do so.

THE HELL TO HEAVEN

Nestled deep in the mountains of China's Anhui Province is Asia's (perhaps the world's) largest test-prep machine, Maotanchang Secondary School or Mao Zhong. More than eleven thousand Mao Zhong students took the college entrance exam in 2013. As in the previous three years, over 82 percent scored above the cutoff point for admission to four-year colleges. Most of the students in the school are not local; the entire population of this remote rural township is only about thirty-five thousand. Students come from other parts of the province and other regions of China. Most are high school graduates who failed to achieve the score needed to get into college or to get into a good college.

The students pay about 48,000 RMB ($6,000) in tuition for one year of study.[37] The 2013 tuition was about the same as the average annual income of residents in Shanghai, China's wealthiest city; twice the average annual income of city residents; and seven times the income of rural residents. With such an expensive price tag comes the opportunity to spend one year in "hell" and the probability of a 100-point increase on next year's *gaokao*. Given that the total possible score on the *gaokao* in Anhui Province was 750 in 2013, a 100-point increase can send many students to college or to a better college than they would have otherwise.

The school has become a legend in China. The national TV network, CCTV, sent a drone to capture the send-off for more than ten thousand students, traveling in seventy buses, escorted by police cars, to take the exam on June 5, 2013. The Mao Zhong model has been used in advertisements by other schools in China in the hope of attracting students. The school has also become a major economic development engine for the township, which traditionally relied on exporting cheap natural resources such as bamboo. Now Mao Zhong has transformed the local economy, creating a boom in real estate and services for the tens of thousands of students and their parents.

The school is a telling example of education in China. It has all the elements that make Chinese education the world's best and worst: hard-working students, devoted parents, well-prepared teachers, efficient instruction, clear goals, high-stakes accountability, and an entire society dedicated to serving the needs of the students.

Parents

Mao Zhong may have the world's most devoted parents. The tuition is not small change, and on top of the tuition are a year's living expenses. Typically one parent, often the mother, comes to live with the student for the entire year. They live in rented rooms or apartments. Demand has driven the average rent up from 5,000 RMB ($900) to 20,000 RMB ($3,300) a year, comparable to rent in far larger cities. In addition, most parents forgo a year's income because they are unable to find employment in the township

As one father, himself a businessman, told his son on successfully enrolling him in the school: "Son, I have made many investments in my life, but you are my biggest. And this investment can only succeed. It is not allowed to fail."

(although many try). Then there are costs for food, supplies, and transportation. But the biggest sacrifice is not financial. Parents have to live apart from the rest of their family, many have to quit their job or put their career on hold for a year, and they must spend that year in a tiny, remote, unfamiliar rural town. Killing time while their children are in school or doing homework is their toughest challenge. But as one father, himself a businessman, told his son on successfully enrolling him in the school: "Son, I have made many investments in my life, but you are my biggest. And this investment can only succeed. It is not allowed to fail."[38]

Students

The workload of Mao Zhong students is three times as heavy as it is in other schools. The number of practice tests students are required to complete in one year is what students in other schools do in three years. To accomplish this, students are required to get up by 6:00 a.m., be in the classroom by 6:30 a.m., and finish the day around 10:30 p.m., when they are released, with homework and preparation still to do for the next day. The concept of the typical week does not apply. A "week" here lasts nine days. On the tenth day come the "weekly" exams. "This is the hell to heaven," one student said.[39]

Teachers

Teachers at Mao Zhong are organized into work units and held accountable as a group. Every year the school appoints a lead teacher for a group of students. The appointment of lead teachers, all of them men, is based on the test scores of their students in the previous year. The bottom few are not appointed. The lead teacher then forms his teaching group by selecting from a pool of teachers who have applied to work with him. The lead teacher is given the authority to fire any member in his teaching group should he find their work unsatisfactory. The performance of the lead teacher and his group are judged entirely by their students' exam scores. A student who scores above the cutoff for prestigious universities earns the group 3,000 RMB in bonus pay. If she or he scores above the cutoff for ordinary universities, the group earns another 2,000 RMB. The money is distributed to the members of the group using a weighted formula. Some teachers receive as much as 50,000 RMB, the equivalent of their annual salary. "The double psychological and financial incentives motivate the over 100 male lead teachers to try all sorts of magic to raise the red number on students exam papers," writes a journalist after visiting the school.[40]

The Township

The town revolves around the school, with almost all of its services catering to the students' needs. In addition to increased housing, the town has seen rapid growth in restaurants, office supply stores, hotels, cell phone services, and agents to help with online shopping. To give the students good luck, the businesses give their services and products names that carry good wishes for academic success. Cell phone cards are called *Zhuangyuan* cards. (*Zhuangyuan* was the title granted to the number one examinee in *keju*.) Hotels and restaurants are named "The Academy." Shops hang banners that say, "Wishing All Students Listed on the Golden Scroll" (which emperors used to announce the winners in *keju*). Moreover, to make sure there are no distractions, the township forbids the establishment of any entertainment outlets. As a result, there is no Internet café, KTV, or video game arcade, and there are none of the billiard saloons popular in many rural small towns. Video surveillance cameras monitor every intersection to prevent students from running around. The whole town quiets at 10:30 p.m. to give the students peace to study and rest.

Teaching

The teaching is strictly exam prep. Anything that does not help raise test scores is considered a distraction and is barred. School leaders are stationed in each teaching building and use video cameras to monitor classroom activities. Teachers can show up anytime in the classroom or in students' rented homes. Students are not allowed to bring electronic devices, food, or drinks to the classroom, nor may they discuss or argue with the teacher in class. One lead teacher told his class on the first day, "You all are here to improve your scores to go to college. So forget your personality and individuality. Do whatever the teachers want you to do. Follow them and you will go to a college."[41]

"The most miserable thing for a teacher is, you have to do things you know are wrong," said one Mao Zhong teacher, speaking on condition of anonymity. Many years ago, the teacher was a fresh graduate of a teachers' college and believed that education should cultivate citizenship. He thus did more than other teachers. For example, he read a collection of essays by a Chinese American author in class and started discussions about love and friendship in his class. Ten years later, a former student thanked him for what he had taught them. What the teacher did not tell his students was that he almost lost his lead teacher appointment that year because his experiments caused a decline in test scores. After that, he stopped his attempts to cultivate the humanities.[42]

BREAKING THE SPELL

The Chinese are extremely aware of the casualties of their exam-oriented education. More than a decade ago, the Chinese Ministry of Education (then the Chinese National Education Commission) officially denounced Chinese education:

> "Exam-oriented education" refers to the factual existence in our nation's education of the tendency to simply prepare for tests, aim for high test scores, and blindly pursue admission rates (to colleges or higher-level schools) while ignoring the real needs of the student and societal development. It pays attention to only a minority of the student population and neglects the majority; it emphasizes knowledge transmission but neglects moral, physical, aesthetic, and labor education, as well as the cultivation of applied abilities and psychological and emotional development; it relies on rote memorization and mechanical drills as the primary approach, which makes learning uninteresting, hinders students from learning actively, prevents them from taking initiatives, and heavily burdens them with excessive amount of course work; it uses test scores as the primary or only criterion to evaluate students, hurting their motivation and enthusiasm, squelching their creativity, and impeding their overall development. "Test-oriented education" violates the *Education Law* and *Compulsory Education Law* and deviates from our education policy. Henceforth, we must take all effective measures to promote "quality education" and free elementary and secondary schools from "test-oriented education."[43]

China has launched a series of reforms over the past thirty years, from massive curriculum reform to governance and financing reforms, from textbook reforms to assessment reforms, and from reforming classroom practices to changing teacher preparation. It has even begun to tinker with the untouchable *gaokao* and college admissions.

Can these efforts succeed?

7

THE WITCH THAT CANNOT BE KILLED
Educational Reforms and Setbacks

Cai Rongsheng was arrested in November 2013 when he tried to travel to Canada via Hong Kong with a fake passport. He reportedly confessed to fraud involving hundreds of millions RMB (tens of millions in US dollars) in his role as the admissions director of Renming University of China or People's University, one of the most prestigious higher education institutions in China since 2003.[1] Although the charge and amount have not been officially released, both the university and the Chinese Ministry of Education have confirmed that Cai "had been under investigation for violation of regulations and illegal conduct."

Cai's arrest set off a firestorm in China's media and cyberspace because it involved an issue that touches almost every Chinese life: college admissions. Generally considered the last frontier of relative fairness and justice in China, college admissions have been tightly regulated by the central government. "Everyone is equal before test scores" is a principle that has been upheld by the standardized *gaokao*, which dictates admission strictly according to students' scores. Thus, college admissions have gained a reputation as almost invulnerable to corruption.

Recent educational reforms, however, are undermining that reputation. By granting universities more autonomy and discretion, reforms are introducing many more opportunities for corruption.

The Chinese government began a grand experiment with the college admissions process in 2001 with the goal of recruiting "students with special talents and innovative potential" who might not score well in all subjects of the *gaokao*. The government allowed a limited number of universities to expand the pool of candidates by lifting the cap.[2] Instead of selecting only from a small candidate pool imposed by a government formula, these universities are allowed to admit from a larger pool of students above the provincial cut score using their own selection criteria. The experiment started with three universities in Jangshu Province in 2001 and has since expanded to about ninety universities across China. Because these universities are prestigious and top-ranked, they have been given more autonomy and discretion in determining who may be admitted. As a result, the experimental universities are some of the most desirable institutions in China.

Increasing an institution's autonomy and discretion makes room for all sorts of variables in addition to test scores. That was and still is the government's intention. By looking at other factors, such as evidence of special talent and creativity, the universities rely less on test scores, and tests would lose their power to determine educational results. But the problem is that other factors are more subjective than test scores, and evidence is obtained in less conventional ways, leaving room for corruption. In the case of Cai, for example, it has been reported that he took bribes for pronouncing some ordinary students "special" in order to admit them.[3] After all, a place at the prestigious People's University is worth a great deal—in some cases, more than 1 million yuan RMB.

The Cai scandal almost derailed China's grand experiment to foster a more diverse and creative workforce. The minute the news broke, the public began questioning the wisdom of the new admissions policy, and some demanded that it be abolished. The People's University did suspend the practice. In December 2013, less than a month after Cai's arrest, the Ministry of Education tightened the rules and issued new regulations.[4] The ministry retracted the earlier policy that allowed certain universities to determine the number of special admissions. Universities could not admit more than 5 percent of their total enrollment using the "autonomous" approach. Other requirements included video-taping the entire interview process, making the university president responsible for the special admissions, and publicizing the results for at least ten days before students are officially admitted.

THE DISASTER OF MAO'S REVOLUTION AGAINST TESTING

China's efforts to free itself from the bondage of exams have been dogged by consequences even more disastrous than corruption. Like its predecessors, the Communist government never stopped working to minimize the influence of exams. One of the most drastic measures the government took was abandoning the college entrance exam entirely during the Cultural Revolution, just as the Qing emperor had done to *keju* in 1905.

The Cultural Revolution, started by Mao Zedong, lasted from 1966 until 1976. That span has been generally condemned as a decade of disastrous political changes, chief among them an educational revolution that dismantled universities and imprisoned scholars. In 1966, the central government postponed the college entrance exam and called for students to "stop classes to participate in the revolution." All school activities were suspended, and teachers from both basic and postsecondary education institutions were sent to labor camps, rural villages, or factories to be reeducated. Those who did not comply became the targets of public criticism and humiliation by students at massive, zealously cruel gatherings. Postsecondary institutions stopped admitting new students and did not resume doing so until 1970.

In 1970, some of the postsecondary schools reopened and began to admit new students, but exam scores were not used as criteria. Instead, students were admitted based on their background and practical experiences. The criteria were political correctness (i.e., alignment with Communist thinking), physical health, a minimum of three years of practical experience, and the equivalent of, at minimum, a middle school education. Workers, peasants, soldiers, and young cadres entered the schools, which had no age limit for those with rich experiences. Students did not have to take entrance exams. Instead, they were recommended by their community, approved by their leaders, and reviewed by the schools. Those admitted were called "worker, peasant, and soldier students." Students with "tainted" family backgrounds—landlords, capitalists, and other "exploitive" classes—had very little chance of being selected.[5]

The reason for this revolution, the damage done by exams, repeats itself in later attempts at reform. Exams have long been considered the source of all evil in China.[6] Mao himself hated test scores and tests. "Testing treats students as enemies and is often launched against them in an ambush," he wrote in 1964. "It works against the active and lively development of youth morally, intellectually, and physically."[7] Mao even cited the great American education philosopher John Dewey to support his revolution: "Opposing direct instruction was advocated by capitalist educationist as early as the May Fourth Movement (in 1919)," said Mao in a published conversation with his nephew Mao Yuanxin, an influential leader in the Cultural Revolution. "Why shouldn't we? The least we can do is not to treat students as objects of attacks."[8] The capitalist educator Mao referred to was John Dewey, who lectured at Peking University in 1919, when Mao was an assistant librarian there.

Exams not only work against the development of individuality and creativity but also prevent equality by limiting the opportunities for the laboring class to gain access to higher education. Test scores and examinations were thus considered counterrevolutionary measures to keep laborers' children away from higher education. In a 1970 article published in the state-controlled paper *People's Daily*, the author argued: "Using test scores as the only measure for college admissions and advocating 'everyone is equal before test scores' is in reality a culture tyranny imposed upon the working people by the capitalist class."[9]

Mao's revolution against tests and test scores went further than removing testing from requirements for college admissions. He wanted to install a new educational paradigm freed from the Confucian and *keju* tradition. He envisioned and forced the implementation of an educational system to serve the masses, not the intellectual elite—the traditional scholars who "never labor their limbs and [are] unable to tell different crops." In Mao's view, education should serve the proletariat, and it should be rooted in their daily activities and experiences. He brought about massive changes: a tremendous expansion of basic education in rural areas, with postsecondary education conducted in factories and villages. Students and teachers labored like peasants and factory workers, academic studies were rendered antirevolutionary, and the required number of years of schooling was reduced.

But Mao's revolution ended shortly after his death in 1976, and the college entrance exam was restored in 1977. The consequences of Mao's revolution have been generally viewed as disastrous. Instead of being allowed to teach, hundreds of thousands of university

Many scholars agree that even though Mao's methods were dictatorial, his intentions to fight against the authoritarianism and intellectualism of Chinese education were well justified.

faculty and leaders were investigated, publicly humiliated, and even tortured. University admissions were completely suspended for four years, resulting in a loss of perhaps 2 million college graduates. The "worker-peasant-soldier students" had extremely low academic capabilities. The quality of teaching in the expanded schools at both the basic and postsecondary level was far from adequate because the teachers did not have adequate preparation. However, Mao's idealistic pursuit of an educational utopia has been reexamined in recent years. Many scholars agree that even though Mao's methods were dictatorial, his intentions to fight against the authoritarianism and intellectualism of Chinese education were well justified.[10]

BACK TO "NAKED" TESTS

Although the entrance exam was restored in 1977, its negative effect on creativity and equality was not lost on the Chinese. A series of policies have since been developed to dilute the power of exams. Initially the government instituted policies to lower the cutoff scores for applicants meeting certain criteria. Up to fifty points could be lowered for students who earned the "Three-Good Student" awards; winners of contests in academic subjects; students with exceptional talents in sports and arts; winners of governmental recognition; and recipients of recognition in other areas.[11] For example, a 1987 policy issue by the Ministry of Education stipulated that high school students who won prizes in provincial-level science and technology invention contests could be admitted with scores lower than the cutoff. Students applying for certain specializations, such as arts, theater, acting, agriculture, forestry, mining, and at one time teacher education, also had a lower cutoff.

After 2001, China began awarding bonus points instead of lowering minimum test scores. College applicants could receive bonuses based on their family background and merits that could not be tested. There are two types of bonuses: compensatory and merit based. Compensatory bonus points are similar in spirit to affirmative action strategies in other countries because these bonus points are intended to compensate for certain disadvantages the students have suffered. For example, students who belong to an ethnic minority group or were educated in areas with a high concentration of ethnic minorities could be awarded points. The second kind of bonus, merit based, was granted to students who had demonstrated desired qualities and talents not easily tested in the college entrance exam: students who received prizes in a national or international contest for scientific and technological invention, students who competed in international Olympiads in math and sciences, and students who competed well in sporting events.

The idea of bonus-point or extra-credit measures was to contain the power of the college entrance exam and recognize students with special talents or interests. However, like the experiment granting autonomy in admissions, these measures have resulted in rampant corruption and created new forms of standardized tests. For example, thirty-one students were found to have faked their ethnicity in Chongqing in 2009, although their ethnic minority status had to be reviewed, inspected, and verified by multiple layers of government agencies.[12] Certification for qualifications of athletic abilities can be bought with a few thousand yuan; so can invention patents. Bribery can bring students honorary titles. According to an investigative report in the national newspaper *China Youth*, assisting students to obtain qualifications for bonus points in the college entrance exam has become a sophisticated industry.[13]

The industry manages bribes and alters ethnicity, and it also includes training centers that prepare students to earn all sorts of certificates and prizes. The Math Olympiad, an international math competition for students, for example, became a de facto mandatory extracurricular activity for virtually all students from the primary grades on up. But it is not math that interests these students. They simply want to win the contest and earn the extra points. Likewise, music, art, and sports have all become ways to earn extra points on the college entrance exam. As a result, music and art classes have turned into exam prep.

The corruption and distortion that entered education when officials tried to foster special talents triggered widespread complaints among the public and leaders alike. Moreover, awarding bonus points to students demonstrating talents in art, music, and sports further disadvantages poor students and students in rural areas because they do not have the same access to these expensive opportunities. Increasingly, people are calling for "naked tests"— that is, using only test scores to make admissions decisions. In response, there has been a dramatic reduction in the number of categories included for extra credit, as well the number of bonus points that can be awarded. Math Olympiad winners, for example, will no longer receive extra points. Neither will winners in some science and technology competitions.

> *Awarding bonus points to students demonstrating talents in art, music, and sports further disadvantages poor students and students in rural areas because they do not have the same access to these expensive opportunities.*

THE WITCH THAT CANNOT BE KILLED

In January 2014, the Chinese Ministry of Education issued a stern policy banning the use of any form of exams for students advancing from primary school to middle school.[14] "Exams cannot be used by local educational administration, government schools, or private schools to select students," stated the policy document. "Government schools cannot use any certificates of contest prizes or qualifications as basis for determining students' eligibility for admissions." For schools with more applicants than space, a computerized lottery is to be used.

This policy is yet another attempt to free Chinese education from the power of exams. Over the past three decades, the Chinese central government and provincial governments have issued similar policies every year. Beginning in the mid-1980s, the central government issued multiple orders forbidding the use of exams in the admission of students to middle schools. All middle schools were required to accept students within their designated communities without using exams to determine eligibility. But in practice, these orders were generally ignored by local governments and schools until the late 1990s. Shanghai began implementing the policy in 1997, and Beijing began a year later.

Officially middle schools are no longer supposed to use formal exams to make admissions decisions and must enroll students residing in their communities. Nor are schools supposed to enroll students from outside their communities, a common way to recruit more academically talented students or increase financial resources by charging a fee to those who are less talented. In reality, both practices continued, forcing central and local governments into an annual exercise of issuing more orders and policies. In 2000, for instance, the Ministry of Education issued an order prohibiting the use of any form of written exams to select students. In 2005, the ministry ordered all government schools to stop offering classes in Math Olympiad and referencing qualifications in Math Olympiad for admissions. In 2006, the Chinese legislature passed the revised Compulsory Education Law, which made using exams to admit students to middle school illegal. In 2009, a similar order was issued again, demanding that schools not give any form of exams and associating admissions with students winning prizes in subject contests. In 2013, the Ministry of Education issued similar orders once more—and again in 2014.

The fact that such orders continue to be issued shows what little effect their predecessors have had. To show compliance, schools and local governments may have stopped formal and open exams, but they have invented new forms of exams or conducted exams without calling them entrance exams. In 2010, a group of middle schools in Sichuan were reported for holding a "scholarship exam," which was to be used for admissions decisions.[15] In 2009, a middle school in Shanxi Province used a commercial tutoring service to conduct its admissions exam. Children who wished to attend the school had to pay to receive tutoring and participate in the exams. The training service could recommend students to the school, and of course, the school happened to admit only students recommended by the service. This type of joint venture has become a popular way for schools to identify the best students and increase revenue, all while evading government scrutiny. A joint venture might offer out-of-school tutoring in the Math Olympiad, English, and other "special talents." These tutoring programs also serve as a selecting mechanism for the middle schools. In addition, while schools are banned from using written exams, they can still conduct interviews, which have become another form of testing.[16]

How is it possible that in such a tightly controlled, authoritarian society, the omnipotent government has been unable to kill the witch of testing?

A 2013 study conducted by the 21st Century Education Research Institute, a Chinese nonprofit think tank, found fifteen different ways for students to advance from primary to middle school in Beijing. Officially there should be only one way: residency in the district. "Invisible and alternative forms of exams have defeated the 'advancing without exams' policy," the study concludes.[17]

"Thus, more than a decade's history of prohibition orders from educational departments has been a history of ineffective orders," notes a report in *China Weekly* after reviewing numerous attempts to curtail the power of testing in Chinese education.[18] How is it possible that in such a tightly controlled, authoritarian society, the omnipotent government has been unable to kill the witch of testing?

ANOTHER WITCH THAT REFUSES TO BE KILLED

Lessening academic burden has been another area of repeated, intensive, yet impotent reforms. The damages caused by an excessive academic burden have long been recognized. Efforts to curtail the time devoted to academic studies and relieve the pressures of school work began in the 1950s, prior to the Cultural Revolution. The first order issued by the Communist government after it took control of China was in 1955, merely six years after the founding the People's Republic of China, or New China.

"The main issue is the excessive amount of homework and testing," noted the Chinese Ministry of Education in 1955. "Students are so occupied with homework and tests that they have to get up early and go to bed late. They cannot even take a nap at noon and must work on Sundays. They are in a constant mode of anxiety and intense pressure." This excessive academic burden resulted "in very bad consequences and severely damaged students' physical and psychological well-being...because they are occupied with rote-memorization...the quality of learning is hard to truly improve." After listing the damages caused by this burden, the Ministry of Education asked that schools take immediate corrective actions to reduce homework and cut back the frequency of testing.[19]

In subsequent years, except during the Cultural Revolution, the Chinese central government has issued about nine similar orders. But the reality has been an increase of academic burdens, not a reduction. Students today are more pressured and spending more time on academic studies than ever before. Nevertheless, the government remains determined to address this issue. So in 2013, the Ministry of Education issued an almost identical order, fifty-eight years after the first one. The 2013 order identified ten actions that schools are required to take:[20]

1. *Transparent admissions.* Admission to a school cannot take into account any achievement certificates or examination results. Schools must admit all students based on their residency without considering any other factors.
2. *Balanced grouping.* Schools must place students into classes and assign teachers randomly. Schools are strictly forbidden to use any excuse to establish fast-track and slow-track classes.
3. *"Zero-starting point" teaching.* All teaching should assume all first-grader students begin at zero proficiency. Schools should not artificially impose higher academic expectations and expedite the pace of teaching.
4. *No homework.* No written homework is allowed in primary schools. Schools can, however, assign appropriate experiential homework by working with parents and community resources to arrange field trips, library visits, and craft activities.
5. *Reducing testing.* No standardized testing is allowed for grades 1 through 3. For fourth grade and up, standardized testing is allowed only once per semester for Chinese language, math, and foreign language. Other types of tests cannot be given more than twice per semester.
6. *Categorical evaluation.* Schools can assess students using only the categories of exceptional, excellent, adequate, and inadequate, replacing the traditional 100-point system.

7. *Minimizing supplemental materials.* Schools can use at most one type of material to supplement the textbook, with parental consent. Schools and teachers are forbidden to recommend, suggest, or promote any supplemental materials to students.

8. *Strictly forbidding extra classes.* Schools and teachers cannot organize or offer extra instruction after regular school hours or during winter and summer breaks and other holidays. Public schools and their teachers cannot organize or participate in extra instructional activities.

9. *A minimum of one hour of physical exercise.* Schools are to guarantee the offering of physical education classes in accordance with the national curriculum, physical activities, and eye exercise during recess.

10. *Strengthening enforcement.* Educational authorities at all levels of government shall conduct regular inspection and monitoring of actions to lessen students' academic burden and shall publish their findings. Individuals responsible for academic burden reduction are held accountable by the government.

As determined as China's government can be, few scholars and parents believe this new order would have any better outcomes than its predecessors. Schools might show token compliance, but the students' burden would not decrease. For example, a school might assign less homework, but parents would then add more. Schools might reduce class time and testing, but parents would send their children to private tutors. In fact, the transfer of burden from within the school to outside the school has been a historical phenomenon. "Whenever the government asks schools to reduce academic burden, tutoring companies are the happiest because more parents come to sign up for their children," observes Xiong Bingqi, deputy president of the 21st Century Education Research Institute.[21]

Here again is the paradox: China's supremely powerful government has been unable to realize its simple wish to reduce the academic burden on students. Actually that's not entirely true, because during the Cultural Revolution, China had no academic burden problem. But that relief came at a high cost: no quality education and massive destruction of educated individuals and educational institutions. As soon as China returned to traditional education, the academic burden returned and quickly became excessive. Now it only seems to get more powerful, despite widespread resentment of its pressures and strong governmental efforts to control it. Why?

THE PRISONER'S DILEMMA

The Chinese government's educational reforms have been compromised by the very people and institutions they were intended to benefit: students, parents, teachers, and schools. Students and parents have long suffered from excessive homework and testing, as have teachers and schools. Talk to any parent, child, and teacher in China, and you will find that very few like the Chinese education system, and an overwhelming majority wants change. But faced with the proposed changes by the government—the very changes the people have demanded—they refuse to cooperate. They are stuck in a game of prisoner's dilemma.

The prisoner's dilemma is a situation in which two individuals choose not to cooperate, even when cooperation could benefit both of them. The classic description of the dilemma is that two individuals are caught for committing a crime and held in separate cells so they cannot communicate with each other. The police offer them each a deal, and they have to make their decision independently. The deal gives each individual four options:

1. If A confesses and B denies committing the crime, A goes free and B goes to prison for ten years.

2. If B confesses and A denies, B goes free and A goes to prison for ten years.
3. If both A and B confess, both go to prison for six years.
4. If both A and B deny, both go to prison for six months.

The best outcome for both is option 4, but the most likely outcome is option 3, as predicated by the Nash equilibrium. Proposed by Nobel laureate John Nash (the movie *A Beautiful Mind* is based on his life), the Nash equilibrium is a concept of game theory. Simply stated, in a Nash equilibrium, "the optimal outcome of a game is one where no player has an incentive to deviate from his or her chosen strategy after considering an opponent's choice. Overall, an individual can receive no incremental benefit from changing actions, assuming other players remain constant in their strategies." [22]

In the classic prisoner's dilemma game, both A and B could choose not to confess to the police (cooperating) and receive a much better payoff for both, but A is mostly likely to assume that B, acting of out his best interest, will choose to confess because that is what he would choose rationally. In this case, A receives a much worse payoff: ten years in prison. So A is likely to choose to confess (defecting). For the same reason, B will choose to confess. Thus both receive a worse payoff: six years in prison instead of six months. In a Nash equilibrium, neither A nor B is likely to change his mind.

In the effort to lessen academic burden and reduce testing, Chinese parents, students, teachers, and schools are all playing

Consequently, although new policies might bring a better education for all, no player in the education game is willing to take the risky first step.

the prisoner's dilemma game. Knowing or assuming that others will continue to do more homework, seek private tutoring, and prepare for tests, very few parents, children, and schools would choose to voluntarily reduce the work load for fear of losing the game. Most schools, knowing that others will continue to use exams to select better students and gain an advantage, will choose to continue to use exams to admit students because the school's reputation is on the line and will be judged by how well its students score in the future. Essentially the dilemma dictates that everyone must continue to behave in the same way. No one can afford to cut back first, for fear that the others won't follow suit. Consequently, although new policies might bring a better education for all, no player in the education game is willing to take the risky first step.

Stuck in their prison, Chinese parents, students, and schools put up a strong resistance to all attempts to reduce academic burden and testing. But in a hierarchically organized society in which the central government holds absolute power, it would seem that subordinate units—local governments and schools—would have to comply or face serious consequences. Indeed, the central government has been serious about enforcing its orders, sending inspection teams and punishing some school principals for violating the orders. To avoid punishment, schools and local governments are forced to come up with creative ways to make the central government believe in their compliance. This need to "fool the emperor" has led to widespread cheating and corruption.

Schools and local governments cannot afford to truly comply with the new rules, for they are all prisoners in the same game. Local government officials have children or grandchildren and their relatives and friends have children and grandchildren, all of whom want to attend a good school. The officials must maintain good relationships with school leaders. As a quid pro quo, local government officials cannot afford to seriously enforce the orders they receive, inspecting schools and delivering harsh punishment to school leaders who are in violation. Instead, the officials often serve as co-conspirators, devising clever ways to show token compliance to fool their superiors. What is damaged—a good education for all in the long term—has little immediate cost to the individual officials, so they are willing to engage in any activities that bring them short-term gains at the cost of the "common good." The result? A tragedy of the commons.[23]

THE TRAGEDY OF THE COMMONS

In a 1968 *Science* article warning about uncontrolled population growth, the late American ecologist Garrett Hardin wrote about the tragedy of the commons. First described by a British amateur mathematician, William Forster Lloyd, the classic scenario of the tragedy of the commons was the ruining of a pasture open to all herdsmen. Acting in his own best interest, each herdsman kept adding more sheep to maximize his own gains. Since the pasture belonged to all, and was hence a commons, adding one more sheep cost the herdsman very little. It seemed a rational, even clever thing to do.

But the capacity of the pasture was limited. And if everyone kept adding, overgrazing would become inevitable. Eventually the pasture would be ruined.

This metaphor has been used in many disciplines to explain the depletion of common resources and destruction of the common good. Overfishing, pollution, and traffic congestion are examples in which individual actors seek to maximize their benefits at the cost of common resources. Spots in China's prestigious educational institutions belong to the government, not to the individual institutions, and thus constitute a commons. These spots are opportunities for both individuals to advance themselves and the nation and its people to achieve prosperity. If the spots go to the right people—a diversity of creative and entrepreneurial talents, as desired by all in China—the society prospers. If not, the commons can be ruined.

The reform efforts in China have been intended to develop a better commons. However, as shown in so many tragedies of the commons, self-interested individuals almost invariably act to gain short-term benefits while ignoring the long-term interests of the commons. The Chinese are no exception. Individual parents and students exert their utmost effort to gain a place in a prestigious institution, studying night and day for the tests, cheating in whatever way possible, and bribing school leaders and admissions officers. As long as students can "graze" on the pasture, they are guaranteed a return: a much better chance to become a civil servant or enter another respectable profession. In addition, as long as graduates enter the civil servant class or take a position in a state enterprise, they will receive social status, power, and material rewards regardless of their ability to perform their job competently. The damage, again, is done to the commons, not to the individual or his or her boss (who works for the state, also a commons).

Schools and officials also have a strong interest in this process. Admitting one poor student, for example, causes little damage to the school or the admissions officer but can bring immediate gains: cash or other forms of quid pro quo. In summary, as long as places in prestigious educational institutions are owned by the government, individuals and local officials aren't likely to act to protect the commons. Instead, they will work to maximize their own interests.

It's possible to avert the tragedy of the commons.[24] One way is regulation that sets rules for individuals accessing the commons. In the past, China has used examinations to determine who receives a place at a prestigious university. But testing obviously does not ensure a healthy commons, so the government has been trying other approaches. Unfortunately those new approaches leave more room for corruption and thus can damage the commons. To avoid corruption, China must continue to rely exclusively on using exams to select students. The Chinese are returning to the idea of using "naked" test scores as the primary regulator—which means China is caught in yet another dilemma that is unlikely to improve its pool of talents.

BREAD AND BUTTERFLY

Mired in these dilemmas, China has found that its efforts to limit the use of exams, reduce academic burden, and grant universities more autonomy in admissions have been rendered ineffective. So have comprehensive reform efforts to broaden the national curriculum, grant more local control of curriculum and textbooks, improve pedagogy, and reduce quality gaps among schools. These efforts, promoted under the general and very vague term of *quality-oriented education* (in contrast to *exam-oriented education*), are only slogans and aspirations. In reality, the essence of Chinese education remains the same as it was ten years ago, twenty years ago, one hundred years, even one thousand years: the system prepares students to

In reality, the essence of Chinese education remains the same as it was ten years ago, twenty years ago, one hundred years, even one thousand years: the system prepares students to pass exams that are believed to lead to a few socially respectable and materially rewarding jobs.

pass exams that are believed to lead to a few socially respectable and materially rewarding jobs.

Effective solutions to China's dilemmas require revolutionary changes to the very foundation on which Chinese society operates. These changes would be so disruptive that they would threaten traditional cultural values and the current social order. Thus they put China in another dilemma—a double bind that is akin to the Bread and Butterfly in Lewis Carroll's *Through the Looking Glass*. This fictional creature Alice encounters has wings made of thin slices of bread, a body made of crust, and a head a lump of sugar. The gnat points out to Alice that the insect is doomed because its only food is hot tea. If it drinks, its head melts. If it does not drink, it faces starvation.

The genesis of Chinese education was the imperial exam, or *keju*, designed to select servants for the emperor, who demanded obedient individuals with a set of homogeneous knowledge and skills. Educational institutions evolved to promote such individuals. By design, they worked to suppress creativity and diversity. Since the emperor controlled the only desirable opportunities for the entire population, anyone who wished to have such opportunities voluntarily subjected himself to the homogenizing process. The concern for both educational institutions and individuals was not how creative and different they could be, but how well they could please the emperor. The only type of creativity rewarded was creativity in pleasing the emperor—in the way in which the emperor wished to be pleased.

Today the emperors are gone, yet China operates very much the same way. The Communist Party has replaced the emperor. Education still serves the same basic purpose: to prepare and select workers for the party and the state. Creative talents are rewarded only when their creativity happens to be desired by the government.

Chinese education is more of a tool for social control than a process for self-enlightenment. The government's interest lies in operating a game that everyone desperately wants to play because then they will willingly comply with all of the demands of the game—in other words, of the government. China has succeeded. By continuing the tradition of *keju*, the gov-

Chinese education is more of a tool for social control than a process for self-enlightenment.

ernment has effectively capitalized on the cultural tradition that shaped the Chinese ethos about education. By controlling the exams, the only way to validate one's worth and thus receive certain rewards, the government has created a game all children must play if they wish to have any chance of living a better life.

The scheme is so perfect that even if the government did not invest in schooling at all, Chinese students and their parents would willingly create educational opportunities on their own, just as their ancestors did. For a long time, the Chinese government's investment in education was abysmal, and even today, it remains low. Parents contribute half of their child's education costs. And if you doubt the success of the education game, just look at how much parents spend on private tutoring.

To perfect this tool of social control, the government dictates the curriculum, even for private schools and universities. Chinese citizens are not allowed to enter international schools in which the Chinese government has no control over the curriculum. Furthermore, all educational institutions, except for the few private ones, are considered branches of the government; thus, teachers and administrators are considered government employees. The Communist Party commissions are the highest governance body in each institution, similar to a school board or board of regents in the United States.

Since the system is intended and designed to induce obedience and compliance, it is not supposed to cultivate truly creative talents. Creative individuals and those who wish to deviate from the government's agenda face tremendous pressure to homogenize. Given the large population, there are always a few who survive the process and remain creative. But those few accidental survivors are not enough to transform China's new economy.

To produce a truly creative citizenry, China cannot just tweak the curriculum or decrease the frequency of exams. It has to abandon the distorted view of education as a tool for social control and begin to accept individual values. Here's how the government could begin:

1. *Give up control of college entrance exams and let individual institutions decide which students to admit.* With a multitude of pathways to success, the gateway to colleges widens, so millions of students do not have to fight for the same narrow entrance. Reduced competition helps alleviates the prisoner's dilemma.

2. *Give up control of educational institutions and allow them to be completely autonomous, governed by locally elected boards.* When institutions are self-governed and autonomous, they are more likely to cherish their own reputation and identity. A spot at a prestigious institution is no longer the commons, but the private territory of that institution. It is now far less likely that university admissions would be corrupted, and this reduces the chance of a tragedy of the commons.

3. *Give up control of what is taught in all schools.* Although the government should provide public educational opportunities, it should not dictate the curriculum for a nation of 1.3 billion. More autonomous institutions have a much better chance of creating diverse and innovative learning opportunities that reflect their identity and their students' strengths. Even if half of the schools fail to cultivate creativity, the other half has a chance. When a nationally uniform curriculum fails, it fails all.

These actions would not necessarily guarantee the production of a creative citizenry because there is still a thousand-year-old cultural tradition to combat. But this new system would have a much better chance than the traditional system. If the Chinese government takes these actions, it will mean the end of an authoritarian regime. If it does not, the hope for Chinese education to produce a truly creative citizenry is very faint.

Drink the hot tea, or starve?

8

THE NAKED EMPEROR
Chinese Lessons for What Not to Do

While China flails, stuck in its Bread and Butterfly dilemma, the rest of the world, oblivious to the struggle, watches in awe. To them, China is an idol. Envy, terror, and genuine admiration—or a mixture of all three—color most outsiders' response to the ancient, gigantic dragon. Its miraculous economic growth, its rapid ascendance on the global political stage, its explosive growth in patent applications and scientific paper output, and its stunning performance on international tests: all of these triumphs seem to suggest that China has found its way to economic growth without following the Western liberal democratic path. At a time when Western democracies are experiencing economic slowdowns and political chaos, the apparent efficiency of China's authoritarian government is an attractive model: an alternative to Western democracy, a threat to the West's complacent superiority, and a fresh source of political, economic, and intellectual inspiration.

But while China's achievements over the past thirty years are laudable, it's a bit premature to declare authoritarianism a victory over democracy. The Chinese economic miracle is not the result of intensified authoritarian control. Rather, it's an involuntary, pragmatic retreat from a rigid totalitarian regime. Suddenly a large population, previously deprived of any autonomy, had the freedom to conduct their daily economic life as they wished. Albeit still very limited, that freedom was enough to enable them to take advantage of an increasingly globalized economy. Alas, as the massive uneducated, cheap, and highly motivated labor force dries up and the world economy changes, China's miracle faces the inevitable challenge of upgrading.

The upgrade will require a different workforce, one that is diverse, creative, and entrepreneurial. But despite 150 years of effort, China has failed to develop an education capable of cultivating such a workforce. Since its humiliating encounters with Western powers in the mid-1800s, China has been on a hesitant journey to develop its people's capacity for scientific and technological innovation. But due to its reluctance to move away from authoritarianism, China's educational philosophy and practice remain as incapable of producing creative and innovative talent as they were two centuries ago. Yet the authoritarian nature of Chinese education has proven extremely effective—at producing great test takers. And so, in a world captivated by test scores, Chinese education rises as a shining, overestimated example.

> *The authoritarian nature of Chinese education has proven extremely effective—at producing great test takers. And so, in a world captivated by test scores, Chinese education rises as a shining, overestimated example.*

Like its economic accomplishment, China's educational achievement is remarkable and respectable. But promoting Chinese education as the world's best is both scientifically inaccurate and philosophically misleading. Much of the world's admiration rests on a simplistic definition of education quality, a romanticized interpretation of the factors contributing to the system's success and an unquestioning glorification of its authoritarian approach. This misplaced admiration leads to China's elevation as a model for the rest of the world, particularly Western countries such as Australia, the United Kingdom, and the United States. While the admiration may be innocent, putting China on a pedestal is dangerous. At best, it will lead to a waste of time and resources, as other countries struggle to copy a model that was proven obsolete over a century ago. At worst, it will destroy the creative Western educational systems that China has been so eager to copy for more than a century. "Chinese education would be a poison for America, not a remedy," warns Saga Ringmar, a Swedish high school student who attended a Shanghai school for two years.[1]

ILLUSIONS OF EXCELLENCE AND EQUITY

The evidence to support China's excellence in education is embarrassingly thin, but it's been well marketed. Given the widespread acceptance of China's peerless status in the world of education, it is mind-boggling to realize that the primary evidence is simply two sets of test scores in three subjects from one source.

China was made the world's model of educational excellence by the Program for International Student Assessment (PISA), the triennial test of fifteen-year-old students in math, reading, and science operated by the Organization for Economic and Cooperative Development (OECD). PISA has become the star maker in the education universe because of its bold claim to assess "the extent to which students near the end of compulsory education have acquired key knowledge and skills that are essential for full participation in modern societies."[2] Moreover, PISA claims to find educational stars by identifying which education systems better prepare their children for "full participation in modern societies" as measured by PISA scores. The goal is for educational systems to learn from "the highest-performing and most rapidly improving school systems."[3]

China was found to have the "strongest-performing" school system in December 2011, when the 2009 PISA results were publicized. Students from Shanghai topped the rankings in all three subjects. A new star had been discovered! The OECD promoted its star with press releases, interviews, blog posts, publications such as *Strong Performers and Successful Reformers in Education: Lessons from PISA for the United States*, and an elaborate video series produced by the Pearson Foundation (in collaboration with PISA and OECD).[4] Shanghai was now officially an education giant, declared the National Center on Education and the Economy (NCEE), a nonprofit education policy think tank in the United States, in a paper, *Standing on the Shoulders of Giants: An American Agenda for Education Reform*, later expanded to a book, *Surpassing Shanghai: An Agenda for American Education Built on the World's Leading Systems*.[5] In addition, a host of reports by international media and awestruck comments by government leaders such as US President Barack Obama and Secretary of Education Arne Duncan gave further credence to China's newly acquired reputation.

It is worth pointing out that none of the publications, media reports, and commentaries provided more empirical evidence. Instead, they simply accepted the illusion of excellence and strengthened it by attempting to explain its causes. The only additional evidence was the same top ranking in the 2012 PISA. Shanghai's fifteen-year-olds again ranked first in all three categories. More promotion and publicity followed, including a report compiled by the NCEE entitled *Chinese Lessons: Shanghai's Rise to the Top of the PISA League Tables*.[6]

The unsuspecting public, along with many national policymakers, have been sold the notion that PISA measures the quality of educational systems; therefore China's is the best. Yet the sole piece of evidence that supports China's status has been critiqued relentlessly. In a June 2013 article in the *Times Education Supplement* magazine, William Stewart raised a barrage of questions:

> But what if there are "serious problems" with the Pisa data? What if the statistical techniques used to compile it are "utterly wrong" and based on a "profound conceptual error"? Suppose the whole idea of being able to accurately rank such diverse education systems is "meaningless", "madness"?
>
> What if you learned that Pisa's comparisons are not based on a common test, but on different students answering different questions? And what if switching these questions around leads to huge variations in the all-important Pisa rankings, with the U.K. finishing anywhere between 14th and 30th and Denmark between fifth and 37th? What if these rankings—that so many reputations and billions of pounds depend on, that have so much impact on students and teachers around the world—are in fact "useless"?[7]

The article's findings are troublesome to PISA and should be extremely unsettling to its faithful, say scholars who have independently reached the same conclusions. "As far as they are concerned, the emperor has no clothes," writes Stewart. Citing numerous publications and conversations with scholars in Denmark, Northern Ireland, and the United Kingdom, as well as with OECD, he points out major technical flaws with PISA's composition of the tests, administering of the tests, and use of statistical techniques to generate country rankings. Stewart uses research by Svend Kreiner, a professor of biomedical statistics at the University of Copenhagen, to point out that the PISA rankings are fundamentally flawed because not all students in each country responded to the same questions. "For example, in Pisa 2006, about half the participating students were not asked any questions on reading and half were not tested at all on maths, although full rankings were produced for both subjects," he writes. Moreover, students in different countries were asked different sets of questions. "Eight of the 28 reading questions used in Pisa 2006 were deleted from the final analysis in some countries."

Kreiner presents a more serious challenge to PISA. He questions the appropriateness of the model PISA uses to produce the country rankings. PISA uses the Rasch model, a widely used psychometric model named after the late Danish mathematician and statistician Georg Rasch. For this model to work properly, certain requirements must be met. But according to Kreiner, who studied under Rasch and has worked with his model for forty years, PISA's application does not meet those requirements. In an article published in the academic journal *Psychometrika*, Kreiner and coauthor Karl Bang Christensen show that the Rasch model does not fit the reading literacy data of PISA, and thus the country rankings are not robust. As a result, rankings of countries can vary a great deal over different subsets. For example, Denmark can rank anywhere between fifth and thirty-sixth out of fifty-six countries.[8] "That means that [PISA] comparisons between countries are meaningless," Kreiner told the *Times Education Supplement*.

Kreiner is not the first or only scholar to raise questions about PISA's technical flaws. In 2007, a collection of nearly twenty researchers from multiple European countries presented their critical analysis in the book *PISA According to PISA: Does PISA Keep What It Promises?*[9] Independent scholars from all over the world took apart PISA's methodology, examining how it was designed; how it sampled, collected, and presented data; and what its outcomes were. Then the researchers compared the test's real-life validity to its claims. Almost all of them "raise[d] serious doubts concerning the theoretical and methodological standards applied within PISA, and particularly to its most prominent by-products, its national league tables or analyses of school systems."[10] Among their conclusions were these:

- ISA is by design culturally biased and methodologically constrained to a degree that prohibits accurate representations of what actually is achieved in and by schools. Nor is there any proof that what it covers is a valid conceptualization of what every student should know.

- The product of most public value, the national league tables, are based on so many weak links that they should be abandoned right away. If only a few of the methodological issues raised in this volume are on target, the league tables depend on assumptions about the validity and reliability which are unattainable.
- The widely discussed by-products of PISA, such as the analyses of "good schools," "good instruction" or differences between school systems...go far beyond what a cautious approach to these data allows for. They are more often than not speculative.[11]

PISA did respond to some of the technical challenges. For example, Andreas Schleicher, PISA's face to the world, wrote a commentary responding to Kreiner's charges in *TES*.[12] While the dispute over PISA's technical flaws continues, some argue that even if PISA did everything right technically, it still could not possibly claim to be measuring the quality of entire education systems, let alone their students' ability to live in the modern world.

Even if PISA did everything right technically, it still could not possibly claim to be measuring the quality of entire education systems, let alone their students' ability to live in the modern world.

"There are very few things you can summarise with a number and yet Pisa claims to be able to capture a country's entire education system in just three of them," wrote Hugh Morrison of Queen's University Belfast in Northern Ireland. "It can't be possible. It is madness."[13]

Morrison, a mathematician, does not think the Rasch model should be used at all. He argues that "at the heart of Rasch, and other similar statistical models, lies a fundamental, insoluble mathematical error that renders Pisa rankings 'valueless' and means that the programme 'will never work.'"[14] The problem of PISA, according to Morrison, violates a central principle of measurement drawn from physicist Niels Bohr's work: the entity measured cannot be divorced from the measuring instrument. Morrison illustrates his point with an example. Suppose Einstein and a student both produced a perfect score on a test. "Surely to claim that the pupil has the same mathematical ability as Einstein is to communicate ambiguously?" The unambiguous communication would be "Einstein and the pupil have the same mathematical ability relative to this particular [test] ... Mathematical ability, indeed any ability, is not an intrinsic property of the individual; rather, it's a joint property of the individual and the measuring instrument."[15] In a nutshell, Morrison's point is that PISA scores students' ability to complete tasks included in the test, not their general ability to understand and succeed.

Even if PISA did measure cognitive abilities as accurately as it claims to, those abilities span only three domains: math, reading, and science. PISA makes the assumption that these skills are universally valuable. In other words, as Svein Sjøberg, a professor of science education at Norway's University of Oslo, points out, PISA "assumes that the challenges of tomorrow's world are more or less identical for young people across countries and cultures" and thus promotes "kind of universal, presumably culture-free, curriculum as decided by the OECD and its experts." This assumption is mistaken. He continues, "Although life in many countries do [sic] have some similar traits, one can hardly assume that the 15-year olds in e.g. Japan, Greece, Mexico and Norway are preparing for the same challenges and need identical life skills and competencies."[16]

Even if cognitive skills in math, science, and reading were the most important skills in the universe, they would not—could not— be the only skills an educational system should cultivate. Skills and knowledge in other domains, such as "the humanities, social sciences, foreign languages, history, geography, physical education etc.," play a crucial role if citizens of any country are to live a fulfilling life.[17] So do noncognitive skills: social-emotional skills, curiosity, creativity, resilience, engagement, passion, and a host of other personality traits. In fact, many would argue that talents, skills, knowledge, and creativity in domains outside math, science, and reading are at least as important, perhaps even more important, to live successfully in the new world. Henry Levin, a professor in economics of education at Teachers College, Columbia University, reviews empirical evidence that shows the essential value of noncognitive skills to work and life in his article "More Than Just Test Scores."[18]

> *Even if cognitive skills in math, science, and reading were the most important skills in the universe, they would not—could not—be the only skills an educational system should cultivate.*

PISA provides no direct evidence of Chinese students' performance in areas beyond math, science, and reading. Thus, even if PISA were methodologically sound, conceptually correct, and properly administered, its only unambiguous conclusion would be that fifteen-year-old students in Shanghai received the highest scores in math, reading, and science in 2009 and 2012. Leaping from the highest PISA score in three subjects to the best education system in the world is too big a jump for any logical person—unless the purpose of education is defined as doing well on the PISA.

Since no one, not the Chinese and not even the PISA team (I hope), would define the purpose of education as achieving good PISA scores, making China the world's model of educational excellence just because some of its fifteen-year-olds received the highest PISA scores is not only inaccurate but misleading. The excellence is a simple illusion created by the PISA league tables.

PISA's operators refuse to have their shiny new star tarnished. In response to doubts about Shanghai's performance, Andreas Schleicher put out a forceful defense in a blog post in 2013.[19] He dismissed critics as narrow-minded, jealous individuals with petty ideas: "Whenever an American or European wins an Olympic gold medal, we cheer them as heroes. When a Chinese does, the first reflex seems to be that they must have been doping; or if that's taking it too far, that it must have been the result of inhumane training."

Schleicher countered charges that the Shanghai sample did not represent children of migrant workers; reiterated that students were not only good at memorization but could also apply their knowledge in math; and stressed that students in Shanghai have more productive beliefs than students in other countries. Schleicher's arguments about the sampling remain controversial. Tom Loveless of Brookings Institute challenged him with more data and evidence, to which PISA has yet to provide an adequate response.[20] Schleicher's statement about Shanghai students' math performance does no more than simply affirm that Shanghai students are the best PISA performers in math. It does not add any more proof that Shanghai has the best education. And his point about Shanghai students' belief that "they will succeed if they try hard and they trust their teachers to help them succeed" does not add proof either. Instead, it confirms that their PISA performance is a result of "inhumane training" and exemplifies Schleicher's and his like-minded observers' attempts to romanticize the insufferable reality Chinese parents and students experience daily.

ROMANTICIZED MISERY

Schleicher has on many occasions promoted the idea that Chinese students take responsibilities for their own learning, while in "many countries, students were quick to blame everyone but themselves." France is his prime example: "More than three-quarters of the students in France ... said the course material was simply too hard, two-thirds said the teacher did not get students interested in the material, and half said their teacher did not explain the concepts well or they were just unlucky." Students in Shanghai felt just the opposite, believing that "they will succeed if they try hard and they trust their teachers to help them succeed." Schleicher maintains that this difference in attitude contributed to the gap between Shanghai, ranked first, and France, ranked twenty-fifth. "And guess which of these two countries keeps improving and which is not? The fact that students in some countries consistently believe that achievement is mainly a product of hard work, rather than inherited intelligence, suggests that education and its social context can make a difference in instilling the values that foster success in education"[21]

Schleicher got the numbers right, but his interpretation is questionable. Plenty of countries that have higher PISA rankings than France report similar attitudes. For example, more students in number eight, Liechtenstein, and number nine, Switzerland (over 54 percent, in contrast to 51 percent in France), said their teachers did not explain the concept well. The percentage of students attributing their math failure to "bad luck" was almost identical across the three countries: 48.6 percent in Liechtenstein, 48.5 percent in Switzerland, and 48.1 percent in France. The difference in percentage of students claiming the course material was too hard wasn't that significant: 62.2 percent in Liechtenstein, 69.9 percent in Switzerland, and 77.1 percent in France. Neither was the difference in the percentage of students saying that "the teachers did not get students interested in the material": 61.8

percent in Liechtenstein, 61.1 percent in Switzerland, and 65.2 percent in France.[22]

Moreover, the PISA report seems to contradict Schleicher's reasoning because it finds that students with lower scores tend to take more responsibility: "Overall, the groups of students who tend to perform more poorly in mathematics—girls and socio-economically disadvantaged students—feel more responsible for failing mathematics tests than students who generally perform at higher levels."[23]

A closer examination of the data reveals that the degree to which students take responsibility for failing in math or blaming outside factors does not have much to do with their PISA performance. Consider the percentage of students who attribute their failing in math to teachers: countries with low percentages of students saying, "My teacher did explain the concepts well this week," or, "My teacher did not get students interested in the material," do not necessarily have the best ranking. Conversely, countries where students are more likely to blame teachers are not necessarily poor performers.

Using Shanghai as the cutoff, the countries with the lowest percentage (below 35 percent) of students blaming their teachers for failing to explain the concepts well are Korea, Kazakhstan, Japan, Singapore, Malaysia, Russian Federation, Chinese Taipei, Albania, Vietnam, and Shanghai-China. An almost identical list of countries has the lowest percentage (below 41 percent) of students blaming their teachers for not interesting students in the material: Kazakhstan, Japan, Albania, Singapore, Thailand, Malaysia, Russian Federation, Montenegro, and Shanghai-China. When the lists are combined, the ten countries with the lowest percentage of students blaming their teachers are Kazakhstan, Japan, Albania, Singapore, Korea, Malaysia, Russian Federation, Chinese Taipei, Shanghai-China, and Vietnam. The countries whose students are most likely to blame their teachers are Norway,

Italy, Germany, Slovenia, France, Austria, the Czech Republic, Sweden, Liechtenstein, and Switzerland.

Among the countries whose students are least likely to blame teachers are some of the best (Shanghai, Japan, Korea, Singapore, Taipei, and Vietnam), worst (Kazakhstan, Albania, Malaysia), and average (Russian Federation) PISA performers. Students who are most likely to blame teachers come from countries that earn the top PISA scores (Liechtenstein, Switzerland, and Germany) and middle-level PISA scores (Norway, Sweden, Italy, Slovenia, France, Austria, and the Czech Republic).

What's intriguing is that the countries whose students are least likely to blame their teachers all have a more authoritarian cultural tradition than the countries whose students are most likely to blame their teachers. On the first list, Singapore, Korea, Chinese Taipei, Shanghai-China, Japan, and Vietnam share the Confucian cultural tradition. And although Japan and Korea are now considered full democracies, the rest of the countries on the list are not.[24] In contrast, the list of countries with the highest percentage of students blaming their teachers for their failures ranked much higher on the Democracy Index. Norway ranked first, Sweden ranked second, and Switzerland was number seven. With the single exception of Italy, all ten countries where students were most likely to blame their teachers ranked above 30 on the Democracy Index (and Italy ranked thirty-second).

One conclusion is easy to draw from this analysis: students in more authoritarian educational systems are more likely to blame themselves and less likely to question the authority—the teacher—than students in more democratic educational systems. An authoritarian educational system demands obedience and does not tolerate questioning of authority. Just like authoritarian parents, authoritarian education systems have externally defined high expectations that are not necessarily accepted by students intrinsically but require mandatory conformity through rigid rules and severe punishment for noncompliance.[25] More important, they work hard to convince children to blame themselves for failing to meet the expectations. As a result, they produce students with low confidence and low self-esteem. On the PISA survey of students' self-concept in math, students in Japan, Chinese Taipei, Korea, Vietnam, Macao-China, Hong Kong-China, and Shanghai-China had the lowest self-concepts in the world, despite their high PISA math scores.[26] A high proportion of students in these educational systems worried that they "will get poor grades in mathematics." More than 70 percent of students in Korea, Chinese Taipei, Singapore, Vietnam, Shanghai-China, and Hong Kong-China, in contrast to less than 50 percent in Austria, United States, Germany, Denmark, Sweden, and the Netherlands, "agreed" or "strongly agreed" that they worry about getting poor grades in math.[27]

In other words, what Schleicher has been praising as Shanghai's secret to educational excellence is simply the outcome of an authoritarian education. As discussed previously, Chinese education has been notoriously authoritarian for thousands of years. In an authoritarian system, the ruler and the ruling class (previously the emperors; today the government) have much to gain when people believe it is their own effort, and nothing more, that makes them successful. No difference in innate abilities or social circumstances matters as long as they work hard. If they cannot succeed, they have only themselves to blame. This is an excellent and convenient way for the authorities to deny any responsibility for social equity and justice and to avoid accommodating differently talented people. It is a great ploy that helped the emperors convince people to accept the inequalities they were born into and obey the rules. It was also designed to give people a sense of hope, no matter how slim, that they can change their own fate by being indoctrinated through the exams.

The ruling class in China has worked diligently to convince people that suffering is good for them and will bring them great success. Mencius, a loyal follower of Confucius who was second only to Confucius in status, wrote over two thousand years ago: "Thus, when Heaven is about to confer a great office on any man, it first exercises his mind with suffering, and his sinews and bones with toil. It exposes his body to hunger, and subjects him to extreme poverty. It confounds his undertakings. By all these methods it stimulates his mind, hardens his nature, and supplies his incompetencies."[28]

Historical tales of hard work that brings success have been passed down for centuries in China; parents and teachers still tell them every day. For example, Sun Jing in the Han dynasty studied day and night. He tied his hair to a beam so that when he fell asleep and dropped his head, the pain would wake him up. He became a successful and famous politician. There was also Su Qin, a well-known minister in the Warring States period (476–221 BC) whose success came from studying hard. To stay awake, he would jab his side with an awl.

Poverty should not matter, Chinese tradition insists. Kuang Heng became the prime minister in the Han dynasty by studying hard, even though he was born in extreme poverty. He could not afford lamp oil, so he made a hole on the wall and studied in the light of his neighbor's lamp. Che Yin, another poor child who could not afford oil, became a powerful government official in the Jin dynasty (265–420); he caught fireflies and put them in a transparent bag to use as a reading light. His contemporary Sun Kang read his books using reflections from the snow.

Accompanying these stories are abundant Chinese sayings about the necessity and possible outcomes of hard work: "Diligence makes up for stupidity"; "Stupid birds get an early start"; "Diligence is the path through mountains of books; suffering is the boat that sails over the ocean of knowledge"; "Only those who could tolerate the bitterest of the bitter can come out as a man above men."

This ploy has been successfully forced on the Chinese people and their children for centuries, and now it is being romanticized by observers such as Andreas Schleicher. "Chinese and Japanese societies allow no excuse for lack of progress in school; regardless of one's current level of performance, opportunities for advancement are always believed to be available through more effort," wrote Harold Stevenson and James Stigler more than twenty years ago in their book *Learning Gap: Why Our Schools Are Failing and What We Can Learn from Japanese and Chinese Education.*[29] In contrast, Americans have been said to hold the assumption that achievement comes from innate ability rather than effort.[30] As a result, it is believed that struggle and tolerance for hardship are valued in China but avoided in the United States.[31]

> *Sold on the idea that effort can trump any inequalities, Chinese parents and schools subject children to extreme hardships, some amounting to child abuse. The controversial book* Battle Hymn of the Tiger Mother *offers a mild version of what a Chinese parent might do to her children.*

Sold on the idea that effort can trump any inequalities, Chinese parents and schools subject their children to extreme hardships, some amounting to child abuse. The controversial book *Battle Hymn of a Tiger Mother* by Yale law professor Amy Chua offers a mild version of what a Chinese parent might do to her children.[32] Following Chua's book came the Chinese *Wolf Dad,* whose motto is "beat the child every three days and they will be admitted to Peking University."[33] Xiao Baiyou, a Chinese businessman, wrote a book sharing the wolf-dad parenting approach that smoothed his three children's way into one of China's top universities. He believes wholeheartedly in the Chinese tradition of education. His children were not allowed to participate in any extracurricular activities. When one showed an interest in studying plants, he said, "You can have your personal interest, but only after you pass the exam to college." He also firmly believes that his children did not need to make any friends before successfully getting into college.

Xiao devised a system with seven principles of beating his children:

1. Beat them less after middle school, but be very strict in early childhood and primary schools.
2. Beat them only with a feather duster, to inflict maximum pain without hurting the bones.
3. Only hit their hands and calves.
4. Lecture before the beating to explain why.
5. Make the other children watch their siblings being beaten.
6. Tell the children in advance how many slashes they will be given and make them count. Each wrong count adds ten more slashes.
7. Children must voluntarily put out their hands to receive the beating and cannot withdraw or cry.

GLORIFIED AUTHORITARIANISM

Xiao's parenting approach is extreme, but like Amy Chua, he received wide attention in China, with hundreds of media interviews, lectures, and book signings. In many ways, his approach is a realization of the "poisonous pedagogy" described by the Swiss psychoanalyst Alice Miller in her book *For Your Own Good*. The basic principles of the "poisonous pedagogy" are as follows:

- Adults are the masters (not the servants!) of the dependent child.
- They determine in godlike fashion what is right and what is wrong.

- The child is held responsible for the adult's anger.
- The parents must always be shielded.
- The child's life-affirming feelings pose a threat to the autocratic adult.
- The child's will must be "broken" as soon as possible.
- All this must happen at a very early age, so the child "won't notice" and will therefor not be able to expose the adults.[34]

According to Miller, this "poisonous pedagogy" was practiced in nineteenth-century Germany and was responsible for producing such authoritarian figures as Adolf Hitler. Its spirit continues today. David Gribble, a British veteran educator and author, translates the principles for educators in his satirical novel *A Really Good School*:

- Teachers are the masters of learners.
- The school determines what is right and wrong.
- The school provides everything that a reasonable parent could desire.
- Children's enthusiasm and curiosity are threats to authority.
- Human behavior is driven by competition.
- The body is disgusting.
- Emotional problems are irrelevant when you are in the classroom.
- If anything goes wrong, it must be the boy's fault.

To implement these principles, Gribble suggests the following methods:

- Unwelcome behavior must be prevented by punishment.
- Teachers must be respected simply because they are teachers, whatever their failings.
- Learners must be humiliated so they become eager to please.
- No teacher must ever show affection for a child.
- Any boy who asks for more must be ignored.
- Boys must be ranked in everything.
- A master must not consider what a boy feels; he only needs to correct what the boy does.[35]

These principles and methods are supposed to be seen in a "school so awful that it could not possibly exist," but such schools do exist, and in great abundance, in China.[36] In fact, the entire Chinese educational system endorses the poisonous pedagogy. At the system level, Chinese education holds that:

- The government (state) is the master of its citizens and by association its children.
- The government (state) determines what is right and wrong.
- The government (state) provides everything that a reasonable parent could desire.
- Children's enthusiasm and curiosity are a threat to authority.
- Human behavior is driven by competition.
- Emotional problems are irrelevant when you are in school.
- If anything goes wrong, it must be the people's fault.

When implemented, these principles translate into:

- A uniform national curriculum
- A high-stakes examination (the college entrance exam)
- A hierarchically organized educational system to implement the curriculum and prepare for the exam
- A tightly controlled, well-trained teaching force to make sure all children comply with what is expected on the exams
- Unsuspecting children and parents forced or drawn to eagerly embrace the precious opportunities doled out, through a miserable and grueling process, by an authoritarian government

These are the features endorsed and celebrated today by Western observers such as Marc Tucker in the book *Surpassing Shanghai*, Thomas Friedman in numerous columns in the *New York Times*, and Andreas Schleicher in his many interviews and writings about the Shanghai miracle. Instead of seeing these features for what they are, powerful ways to control people, these pundits want Western countries to emulate China's traditions simply because they are the secret to Shanghai's PISA performance.

WHY NOT EMULATE SHANGHAI?

It is almost absurd that this book needs to be written and this question asked, because for over a century, China has been trying to reject its own educational system and replace it with the education that produced the more developed economies in the West. But the question does need to be raised because of the widespread misinformation about Chinese education, the seductive misinterpretation of China's economic and educational achievements, and the misguided popular recommendations for Western democracies to copy China.

No one would disagree that the world needs excellence in education. But what defines excellence? There are two paradigms: employee oriented and entrepreneur oriented.[37] While both aim to prepare children to live successfully, the former focuses on transmitting a body of knowledge and skills predetermined to be valuable, and the latter emphasizes developing the potential of each individual child. The former presumes that the necessary knowledge and skills can be determined by predicting the needs of the society and the economy, while the latter assumes that a child whose potential is developed will become valuable in her own way. Employee-oriented education values what children *should* learn, while entrepreneur-oriented education values what children *would* learn. Employee-oriented education prepares children to fit existing jobs, while entrepreneur-oriented education prepares children to take the responsibility of creating jobs.

Excellence in one paradigm does not mean excellence in the other. Quite the contrary. When a school or system becomes extremely good at preparing employees, it is not necessarily good at preparing entrepreneurs, because different paradigms lead to different arrangements of educational institutions and systems. Given its primary goal to efficiently and effectively transmit pre-determined knowledge, the employee-oriented education para-digm requires an apparatus with clearly defined learning outcomes for all students, well-trained teachers knowledgeable about the content to be transmitted and skilled at doing so, engaged stu-dents willing and able to learn the content, standardized mea-sures to monitor the progress of each student and institution, and other resources aligned with the prescribed content. Uniformity, consistency, standardization, competition, data-driven practices, and an emphasis on outcomes are the features of employee-oriented education.

In distinct contrast, entrepreneur-oriented edu-cation maximizes individual differences. Schools follow-ing this paradigm have no standardized, common cur-riculum. Each child pursues his or her interests and pas-sions, and teachers respond to and support those indi-vidual pursuits and assess students' progress accord-ingly. Variation, diversity, tolerance (or indulgence), autonomy, and student-driven educa-tion are features of entrepreneur-oriented education.

Variation, diversity, tolerance (or indulgence), autonomy, and student-driven education are features of entrepreneur-oriented education.

Today the world's measure of excellence in education follows the old paradigm. Excellence is defined as effectiveness and efficiency in homogenizing children and transmitting the pre-scribed content, indicated by standardized test scores in a few subjects. Schools and nations that produce higher test scores are considered to have better educational systems. Hence China has been made the model of excellence.

But it is an excellence of the past.

To cultivate the talents we need for the twenty-first century, we must redefine excellence in education. Instead of effectiveness in homogenizing students, an excellent education should support the development of diverse talents. Instead of suppressing creativity and individual differences, an excellent education should deliberately encourage and shape them. Instead of preparing compliant employees, an excellent education should intentionally encourage children to be entrepreneurial. Instead of overemphasizing global competitiveness, an excellent education should foster a global perspective. Excellence in education should thus be measured by its effectiveness in providing personalized education that promotes diversity and creativity, engaging children in global interactions, and inspiring entrepreneurship and innovation.[38]

Chinese education is the complete opposite of what we need for the new era.

First, the educational excellence in Shanghai is no more than an illusion. The primary evidence that has been used to support the claim that Shanghai has an excellent education is its students' PISA scores in three subjects. Given the exam's technical problems and compared to the true purpose of a modern education, these scores are hardly evidence of greatness. Tucker, Friedman, and other like-minded observers have been trying to offer lessons about "Shanghai's rise to the top of the PISA league tables."[39] In reality Shanghai has not risen to the top. It already stood at the top in 2009, the first time it participated in PISA. If Shanghai's students had taken the PISA in 2000, they would have made top scores then as well, because the magical ingredients have been present for thousands of years. So unless PISA scores are the ultimate goal of education, there is no reason to admire, envy, or copy education in China.

Second, behind the illusion of excellence is an insufferable reality that the Chinese have long been trying to escape. Historical and contemporary evidence, as presented in previous chapters, suggests that the Chinese education stifles creativity, smothers curiosity, suppresses individuality, ruins children's health, distresses students and parents, corrupts teachers and leaders, and perpetuates social injustice and inequity. In other words, what has given China its stunning PISA scores has cost China dearly. The authoritarian education system and tradition are at least partially responsible for the humiliating military defeats by Western powers in the 1900s; the slow development of scientific and technological innovations over the past century; and the shortage of innovative and creative talents China needs desperately if it is to transform its economy into one that is productive and innovation driven. The Chinese have long recognized the damages of their education system and have taken drastic actions to change it for over a century, but they have had little success. China continues to struggle with traditions that appear to be mechanisms for excellence, yet hold China back from any real, meaningful change.

Third, at the core of Chinese education are the three basics that Zhang Mingxuan, China's PISA director, uses to explain Shanghai's success: Chinese families' high expectations, hard work and diligence, and the examination system. As we've seen, the high value Chinese parents place on education is simply a survival strategy to cope with an authoritarian regime. Since all other possibilities for success have been removed by the authoritarian regime, education—or, rather, test preparation—is the only path to success.

Chinese students' diligence is the result of an ancient ploy designed to deny the existence of social injustice and individual differences and suppress individuals' desire to question authority and demand equality. Hard work, effort, and struggle are of course important for both learning and life, but denying the important influence of human nature and family conditions can

Chinese students' diligence is the result of an ancient ploy designed to deny the existence of social injustice and individual differences and suppress individuals' desire to question authority and demand equality.

do great damage. One consequence is the vast inequality of opportunities. The likelihood of attending a college is much higher for a child born in an urban area than for a child born in a rural village, even if the child in the village works harder than his urban peer.[40] Another damaging consequence is the loss of great talents. Hard work can help with rote memorization and preparing for exams, but for true creative and innovative work, one needs passion, interest, and some innate strength. Moreover, the belief that everyone can succeed the same way as long as they work hard has led to the virtually complete negligence of children with disabilities and special needs.

Zhang calls the exam, or *gaokao*, a great equalizer. It may appear so, because it seems that test scores are the only incorruptible measure in China. However, the *gaokao*, like any other exam of that nature, is inherently discriminatory, favoring those who have the resources to prepare, the propensity to do well, and the interest in what is being tested, and working against those who are unwilling or unable to comply.

These elements are intuitively seductive and very difficult to undo. Unless the West wishes to be stuck with a system that cannot be easily broken, it is best not to use China as a model.

Education in the West must go through transformative changes. A paradigm shift will be necessary if teachers are to prepare children to live successfully in the new world.[41] As traditional routine jobs are offshored and automated, we need more and more globally competent, creative, innovative, entrepreneurship-minded citizens who are job creators instead of employment-minded job seekers. To cultivate new talents, we need an education that enhances individual strengths, follows children's passions, and fosters their social-emotional development. We do not need an authoritarian education that aims to fix children's deficits according to externally prescribed standards.

China's education represents the best of the past. It worked extremely well for China's imperial rulers for over a thousand years, but it stopped working when the modern world emerged. It continued to produce students who excel in a narrow range of subjects. But these students lack the very qualities the new society needs. This is why only 10 percent of Chinese college graduates are found to be employable by multinational businesses.[42]

In no way can China serve as the model for the future. In fact, we don't yet have a model that will meet the needs of a global future.

We will have to invent one.

NOTES

Introduction: Fatal Attraction

1. "Atlanta School Leader Beverly Hall Named 2009 National Superintendent of the Year," press release, American Association of School Administrators, February 29, 2009, http://www.aasa.org /content.aspx?id=1592.

2. "American Educational Research Association Presents Annual Awards," May 2, 2010, http://www.aera.net/Portals/38/docs /News_Media/News%20Releases%202010/Annual%20 Meeting%20Awards.pdf.

3. "Grand Jury Indicts 35 in Connection with Atlanta Public Schools Cheating Scandal," media alert, Office of the Fulton Country District Attorney, March 29, 2013, http://www.11alive.com/assetpool /documents/130329074503_APS-Indictment-Announcement.pdf.

4. A *USA Today* investigative report in 2011 revealed over sixteen hundred cases of cheating in six states and Washington, DC. Greg Toppo, Denise Amos, Jack Gillum, and Jodi Upton, "When Test Scores Seem Too Good to Believe," *USA Today*, March 17, 2011, http://usatoday30.usatoday.com/news/education/2011–03–06 -school-testing_N.htm.

5. Sharon Nichols and David Berliner, *Collateral Damage: How High-Stakes Testing Corrupts America's Schools* (Cambridge, MA: Harvard Education Press, 2007).

6. Diane Ravitch, *The Death and Life of the Great American School System: How Testing and Choice Are Undermining Education* (New York: Basic Books, 2010).

7. "Secretary of Education 'Stunned' by Scandal," *11 Alive,* July 6, 2011, http://www.11alive.com/news/article/196896/40/Secretary-of -Education-stunned-by-scandal?__hstc=215845384.d6c6693f407f 802334dab4314f40436c.1365186589630.1365186589630 .1365186589630.

8. "Atlanta School Leader Beverly Hall Named 2009 National Superintendent of the Year."

9. Michael Winerip, "A New Leader Helps Heal Atlanta Schools, Scarred by Scandal," *New York Times,* February 20, 2012, http:// www.nytimes.com/2012/02/20/education/scarred-by-cheating -scandal-atlanta-schools-are-on-the-mend.html?pagewanted=all.

10. Claudio Sanchez, "El Paso Schools Cheating Scandal: Who's Accountable?" *NPR,* August 10, 2013, http://www.npr.org/2013 /04/10/176784631/el-paso-schools-cheating-scandal-probes -officials-accountability.

11. Patrick Michaels, "Faking the Grade: The Nasty Truth behind Lorenzo Garcia's Miracle School Turnaround in El Paso," *Texas Observer,* October 31, 2012, http://www.texasobserver.org/faking -the-grade-the-nasty-truth-behind-lorenzo-garcias-miracle-school -turnaround-in-el-paso/.

12. M. Tucker, *Chinese Lessons: Shanghai's Rise to the Top of the PISA League Tables* (Washington, DC: National Center on Education and the Economy, 2014); K.-M. Cheng, "Shanghai: How a Big City in a Developing Country Leaped to the Head of the Class," in *Surpassing Shanghai: An Agenda for American Education Built on the World's Leading Systems,* ed. M. S. Tucker (Cambridge, MA: Harvard Education Press, 2011), 21–50.

13. Andreas Schleicher, "Are the Chinese Cheating in PISA or Are We Cheating Ourselves?" *OECD Education Today,* December 30, 2013, http://oecdeducationtoday.blogspot.com/2013/12/are-chinese -cheating-in-pisa-or-are-we.html.

14. M. Tucker, ed., *Surpassing Shanghai: An Agenda for American Education Built on the World's Leading Systems* (Cambridge, MA: Harvard Education Press, 2011).

15. Y. Zhao, *World Class Learners: Educating Creative and Entrepreneurial Students* (Thousand Oaks, CA: Corwin, 2012).

16. D. Farrell and A. J. Grant, *China's Looming Talent Shortage* (New York: McKinsey and Company, 2005).

17. Nicolas Boulanger, quoted in J. D. Spence, *The Search for Modern China* (New York: Norton, 1990), 134.

Chapter 1: Fooling China, Fooling the World

1. Sun Yat-sen was an alumnus of President Barack Obama's alma mater, Punahou School in Hawaii.

2. Noel Pugach, "Embarrassed Monarchist: Frank J. Goodnow and Constitutional Development in China: 1913–1915," *Pacific Historical Review* 42, no. 4 (1973): 499–517, 504–505.

3. "Embarrassed Meritocrats," *Economist,* October 27, 2012, http://www.economist.com/news/china/21565228-westerners-who-laud-chinese-meritocracy-continue-miss-point-embarrassed-meritocrats.

4. Pugach, "Embarrassed Monarchist," 508.

5. Ibid., 506.

6. Joshua Kurlantzick, *Democracy in Retreat: The Revolt of the Middle Class and the Worldwide Decline of Representative Government* (New Haven, CT: Yale University Press, 2013).

7. Thomas Friedman, *Hot, Flat, and Crowded: Why We Need a Green Revolution—and How It Can Renew America* (New York: Farrar, Straus & Giroux, 2008). *Meet the Press,* transcript for May 23, 2010, http://www.nbcnews.com/id/37279599/ns/meet_the_press/page/4/#.UZBBjStgZnA/.

8. Ibid.

9. Thomas Friedman, "Our One-Party Democracy," *New York Times,* August 16, 2010, http://www.nytimes.com/2009/09/09/opinion/09friedman.html?_r=2&.

10. The three books are *The World Is Flat: A Brief History of the Twenty-First Century* (New York: Farrar, Straus & Giroux, 2005); *Hot, Flat, and Crowded: Why We Need a Green Revolution—and How It Can Renew America;* and *That Used to Be Us: How America Fell Behind in the World It Invented and How We Can Come Back* (New York: Picador, 2011).

11. China Passes Germany in Economic Rankings," *CNN.com/asia*, January 15, 2009, http://edition.cnn.com/2009/WORLD/asiapcf /01/15/china.economy/.

12. "China Overtakes Japan as World's Second-Biggest Economy," Bloomberg.com, August 16, 2010, http://www.bloomberg.com /news/2010–08–16/china-economy-passes-japan-s-in-second -quarter-capping-three-decade-rise.html.

13. "OECD Report Says China's Economy Will Overtake US Economy by 2016, *International Business Times*, March 22, 2013, http:// www.ibtimes.com/oecd-report-says-chinas-economy-will -overtake-us-economy-2016–1146333.

14. Joshua Cooper Ramo, *The Beijing Consensus*. (London: Foreign Policy Center, 2004), 4.

15. Ibid., 2.

16. Ibid., 3.

17. Ibid., 4.

18. Michael Elliott, "China Takes on the World," *Time*, January 11, 2007.

19. Joshua Kurlantzick, *Charm Offensive: How China's Soft Power Is Transforming the World* (New Haven, CT: Yale University Press, 2008).

20. Joseph S. Nye, *Soft Power: The Means to Success in World Politics* (New York: Public Affairs, 2004).

21. Martin Jacques, *When China Rules the World: The End of the Western World and the Birth of a New Global Order* (New York: Penguin, 2009).

22. Stefan Halper, *The Beijing Consensus: Legitimizing Authoritarianism in Our Time* (New York: Basic Books, 2012).

23. Joshua Kurlantzick, *Democracy in Retreat: The Revolt of the Middle Class and the Worldwide Decline of Representative Government* (New Haven, CT: Yale University Press, 2013), 120.

24. Marc Tucker, ed., *Surpassing Shanghai: An Agenda for American Education Built on the World's Leading Systems* (Cambridge, MA: Harvard Education Press, 2011).

25. Harold M. Stevenson and James W. Stigler, *The Learning Gap: Why Our Schools Are Failing and What We Can Learn from Japanese and Chinese Education* (New York: Simon & Schuster, 2006).

26. Sam Dillon, "Top Test Scores from Shanghai Stun Educators," *New York Times*, December 7, 2010, http://www.nytimes.com/2010/12 /07/education/07education.html?pagewanted=1&_r=2.

27. Sean Coughlan, "China: The World's Cleverest Country?" *BBC News*, May 8, 2012, http://www.bbc.com/news/business-17585201.

28. Michael Gove, "Michael Gove: My Revolution for Culture in Classroom," *Telegraph*, December 28, 2010, http://www .telegraph.co.uk/education/8227535/Michael-Gove-my-revolution -for-culture-in-classroom.html.

29. Richard Adams and Jessica Shepherd, "Michael Gove Proposes Longer School Day and Shorter Holidays," *Guardian*, April 19, 2013, http://www.theguardian.com/politics/2013/apr/18/michael-gove -longer-school-day-holidays.

30. Steve Connor, "US Science Chief Warns: 'China Will Eat Our Lunch,'" *Independent.* November 25, 2011, http://www.independent .co.uk/news/science/us-science-chief-warns-china-will-eat-our -lunch-2219974.html.

31. Taifeng Shu, *Zhongguo Jujue Pengsha [China refuses to be killed by flattery]* (Beijing: Zhongguo Gongshanglian Chubanshe, 2011).

32. Yang Jiechi, opening remarks at the 2013 US-China Strategic and Economic Dialogue, Washington, DC, July 7, 2013, http://www.gov .cn/ldhd/2013–07/12/content_2445559.htm.

33. Pew Research Center, "US Public, Experts Differ on China Policies: Public Deeply Concerned about China's Economic Power," September 18, 2018, http://www.pewglobal.org/2012/09/18 /u-s-public-experts-differ-on-china-policies/.

34. Martin Jacques, "How China Will Change the Global Political Map," *Transatlantic Academy*, March 2013, http://www.transatlanticacademy .org/sites/default/files/publications/Jacques_GlobalPoliticalMap _Mar13.pdf.

35. Joseph Nye Jr., "China's Rise Doesn't Mean War," *Foreign Policy*, January 2, 2011, http://www.foreignpolicy.com/articles/2011/01 /02/unconventional_wisdom.

36. Daniel W. Drezner, "…and China Isn't Beating the U.S.," *Foreign Policy*, January 2, 2011, http://www.foreignpolicy.com/articles/2011 /01/02/unconventional_wisdom.

Chapter 2: The Emperors' Game

1. H. B. Pak, *China and the West: Myths and Realities in History* (Leiden, Netherlands: E. J. Brill, 1974), 55.
2. Ibid.
3. Ibid.
4. Ibid.
5. A. H. Rowbotham, "Voltaire, Sinophile," *PMLA* 47 (1932): 1050–65.
6. Ibid.
7. A. R. Davis, "The Character of a Chinese Scholar-Official as Illustrated by the Life and Poetry of T'ao Yuan-Ming," *Arts: The Journal of the Sydney University Arts Association* 1, no. 1 (1958): 37.
8. K. Winston, "Advisors to Rulers—or, What the Kennedy School of Government Can Learn from Chinese Scholar-Officials, and Vice Versa," working paper, Harvard Kennedy School of Government, Cambridge, MA, 2005.
9. Ibid., 3.
10. Y. Sun, *Wuquan xianfa* [The five-power constitution], March 20, 1921, http://zh.wikisource.org/wiki/%E4%BA%94%E6%AC%8A%E6%86%B2%E6%B3%95.
11. Weiwei Zhang, "Meritocracy, versus Democracy," *New York Times*, November 9, 2012, http://www.nytimes.com/2012/11/10/opinion/meritocracy-versus-democracy.html?_r=0.
12. More information about this series can be found at http://en.wikipedia.org/wiki/Science_and_Civilisation_in_China.
13. J. Y. Lin, "Needham Puzzle, Weber Question and China's Miracle: Long Term Performance since the Sung Dynasty" (paper presented at the World Economic Performance: Past, Present and Future—Long Term Performance and Prospects of Australia and Major Asian Economies, 2006), http://www.uq.edu.au/economics/cepa/docs/seminar/papers-nov2006/Lin-Paper.pdf.
14. Ibid.
15. Ibid., 12–13.
16. J. K. Fairbank and M. Goldman, *China: A New History* (Cambridge, MA: Harvard University Press, 2001), 360.
17. E. Backhouse and J. O. P. Bland, *Annals and Memoirs of the Court of Peking* (Boston: Houghton Mifflin, 1914), 325.

18. G. Li, "Feichu Keju Bainian" [A century after the demolition of keju], 2005, http://news.xinhuanet.com/comments/2005–08/29/content_3415631.htm.

19. W. Hu, *Dizhi de Zhongjie* [The end of imperial rule] (Beijing: Zhongguo Dangdai Chubanshe, 2011).

20. Li, *Feichu Keju Bainian.*

Chapter 3: Governance without Governing

1. T. C. Fishman, *China Inc.: How the Rise of the Next Superpower Challenges America and the World* (New York: Scribner, 2005), 44.

2. G. Chen and C. Wu, *Xiaogangcun de Gushi* [Stories of Xiaogang Village] (Beijing: Huawen Chubanshe, 2009).

3. X. Deng, *Deng Xiaoping Wenxuan Disanjuan [Selected works of Xiaoping Deng]* (Beijing: Renming Chubanshe, 1993), 237.

4. H. Angang, H. Linlin, and C. Zhixiao, "China's Economic Growth and Poverty Reduction (1978–2002)" (paper presented at A Tale of Two Giants: India's and China's Experience with Reform and Growth, meeting of the International Monetary Fund and National Council of Applied Economic Research, New Delhi, 2003), http://www.imf.org/external/np/apd/seminars/2003/newdelhi/angang.pdf.

5. Chen and Wu, *Xiaogangcun de Gushi.*

6. X. Wu, *Jidang Sanshi Nian* [Thirty years of reform] (Beijing: Zhongxin Chubanshe, 2008).

7. Deng Xiaoping's speech on his 1992 tour of the south. Available in Chinese at http://business.sohu.com/20120113/n332115956.shtml.

8. P. Song, "Nian Guangjiu: Shui ye Wufa Daiti de Geshi Jingji Biaobeng Renwu" [Nian Guangjiu: An irreplaceable specimen of private enterprises], *Chutian Xinwen Guangbo*, 2008, China.com.cn, 2008.

9. Q. Xu, "Siying Jingji Shi Zengme Huode 'Zhunshengzheng' de" [How private economy received its legal status], April 30, 2007), http://theory.people.com.cn/GB/49154/49155/5689522.html.

10. Anup Shah, "Poverty around the World," *Global Issues*, November 12, 2011, http://www.globalissues.org/article/4/poverty-around-the-world#WorldBanksPovertyEstimatesRevised.

11. X. Zhang, "Woguo Getihu Shoupo 4000 Wan Hu" [Getihu in China exceeds 40 million for the first time], February 16, 2003, http://finance.chinanews.com/cj/2013/02–16/4564431.shtml.

12. Sophie Song, "China Now Has More Than 260 Million Migrant Workers Whose Average Monthly Salary Is 2,290 Yuan ($374.09)," *International Business Times*, May 28, 2013, http://www.ibtimes.com/china-now-has-more-260-million-migrant-workers-whose-average-monthly-salary-2290-yuan-37409–1281559.

13. J. Y. Lin, *Needham Puzzle, Weber Question and China's Miracle: Long Term Performance since the Sung Dynasty*, in *World Economic Performance: Past, Present and Future—Long Term Performance and Prospects of Australia and Major Asian Economies* (Brisbane, Australia: School of Economics, University of Queensland, 2006).

14. Deng, *Deng Xiaoping Wenxuan Disanjuan*, 238.

15. Confucius, *Lun Yu* [Analects of Confucius] (Adelaide, Australia: University of Adelaide, 2012). *Shun* was a legendary leader in ancient China, around the twenty-third to twenty-second century BC. He has been considered one of the greatest leaders in Chinese history.

16. R. W. Belk and N. Zhou, "Learning to Want Things," *Advances in Consumer Research* 14 (1987): 478–81.

17. L. Ma, *Jiaofeng: Gaige Kaifang Sici Dazhenglun Qingliji* [Thirty years of battle: Personal experiences with the four great debates of reform and opening-up] (Nanjing, China: Jiangsu Reming Chubanshe, 2008).

18. Ibid.

19. Ibid.

20. Paul Krugman, "Hitting China's Wall," *New York Times*, July 18, 2013, http://www.nytimes.com/2013/07/19/opinion/krugman-hitting-chinas-wall.html?_r=0.

21. Michael Schuman, "The Real Reason to Worry about China," *Time*, April 28, 2013, http://business.time.com/2013/04/28/the-real-reason-to-worry-about-china/#ixzz2Zd2Wjxnr.

22. Stephen Leeb, "Paul Krugman Is as Wrong about China as He Was about Singapore," *Forbes*, July 23, 2013, http://www.forbes.com/sites/greatspeculations/2013/07/23/why-paul-krugman-is-wrong-about-china/.

23. Y. Wang, "Zhengque kandai Zhongguo jingji de xiaxian shangxia he dixian" [View in proper perspective the Chinese economy's lower limit, upper limit, and bottom line], July 21, 2013, http://news.xinhuanet.com/fortune/2013–07/21/c_125041239.htm.

24. Y. Liu, C. Lou, and Y. Ding, "Zhuanfang caizhengbu buzhang Lou Jiwei" [Interview with Minister of Finance Lou Jiwei], July 20, 2013, http://news.xinhuanet.com/fortune/2013–07/20/c_116620885.htm.

25. C. Li, "Ruhe zhengque kandai he bawo dangqian gongguan jingji zhengce kuangjia" [How to properly view and grasp the current macroeconomic policy framework], July 22, 2013, http://news.xinhuanet.com/fortune/2013–07/22/c_125041270.htm.

26. W. Shen, "Zongli tongchou Zhongguo jingji shengji" [Chinese premier to coordinate the economic upgrade], July 24, 2013, http://news.xinhuanet.com/fortune/2013–07/24/c_125055248.htm.

27. M. Liang and M. Tan, "Meiti: Zuigaoceng dazao jingji shengjiban, Zhongguo jiang yinglai 'huangjin shidai'" [Media: High-level leadership to build an upgraded version of economy, China welcomes the "Golden Age"], July 24, 2013, http://finance.ifeng.com/a/20130724/10247422_0.shtml.

28. H. Zhen, "Zhenzheng ba chuangxin qudong fazhan zhanlue luodao shichu" [Truly realize the innovation-driven development strategy]," *Liaowang Zhoukang* [Outlook weekly], July 29, 2013.

Chapter 4: Hesitant Learner

1. S. Bieler, *"Patriots" or "Traitors"? A History of American-Educated Chinese Students* (New York: East Gate, 2004); L. Leibovitz and M. Miller, *Fortunate Sons: The 120 Chinese Boys Who Came to America, Went to School, and Revolutionized an Ancient Civilization* (New York: Norton, 2012); E. J. M. Rhoads, *Stepping Forth into the World: The Chinese Educational Mission to the United States, 1872–81* (Hong Kong: Hong Kong University Press, 2011).

2. G. Qian and J. Hu, *Daqing Liumei Youtong Ji [Chinese Educational Commission students]* (Beijing: Dangdai, 2010), 75.

3. J. A. Litten, *American-Educated Chinese Students and Their Impact on U.S.-China Relations* (Williamsburg, VA: College of William and Mary, 2009).

4. T. T. Woo, "Chinese Educational Commission," *Hartford Daily Courant*, April 1, 1880, http://www.colebrookhistoricalsociety.org /PDF%20Images/Chinese%20Educational%20Mission.pdf.

5. Z. Tian, *Zhongguo Jiaoyushi Yanjiu: Jindai Fengjuan [Study of Chinese education history: Modern period]* (Shanghai, China: East China Normal University Press, 2009), 42.

6. J. K. Fairbank and M. Goldman, *China: A New History* (Cambridge, MA: Harvard University Press, 2001), 213.

7. Ibid., 217–18.

8. Tian, *Zhongguo Jiaoyushi Yanjiu*, 29.

9. Fairbank and Goldman, *China: A New History*, 217.

10. Ibid.

11. Ibid.

12. Bieler, *"Patriots" or "Traitors"?*

13. Fairbank and Goldman, *China: A New History*, 404.

14. The Boxer Indemnity Scholarship Program was a scholarship program funded by the indemnity money paid by the Chinese government to the United States. In the aftermath of the Boxer Rebellion, US Secretary of State John Hay had suggested that the $30 million plus Boxer indemnity paid to the United States was excessive. After several negotiations, President Theodore Roosevelt obtained congressional approval in 1909 to reduce the Qing government indemnity payment by $10.8 million, on the condition that the fund was to be used as scholarship for Chinese students to study in the United States. The program supported over a thousand students, many of whom became influential scientists, engineers, and social leaders.

15. Y. Jiang, "Jiaoyu daguo de jueqi: Gaibian guojia mingyun de zhanlue jueze" [The rise of a powerful nation of education: Life changing strategic decisions], October 7, 2008, http://edu.people.com.cn /GB/8137271.html.

16. G. Ma, "Jin Guantao: Bashi niandai de yige hongda sixiang yundong" [Jin Guantao: A grand intellectual movement of the 1980s], April

27, 2008, http://finance.sina.com.cn/review/essay/20080427
/11264806521.shtml.

17. X. Deng, *Deng Xiaoping Wenxuan Disanjuan* [Selected works of
Xiaoping Deng] (Beijing: Renming Chubanshe, 1993), 195.

18. X. Su and L. Wang, *Heshang* [River elegy] (Beijing: Xiandai
Chubanshe, 1988), 98–99.

19. Editorial Team of Biography of Wang Zhen, *Wang Zhen Zhuan*
[Biography of Wang Zhen] (Beijing: Dangdai Zhongguo Chubanshe,
2001).

20. Bao Tong and Chen Yizhi were two of Zhao Ziyang's top aides and
were viewed as supporters of the liberation movement. Bao was
sentenced to prison after the Tiananmen Square crackdown, and
Chen escaped to the United States.

21. *Shanran* means that a living monarch willingly passes the throne to
a younger and more capable successor, regardless of his background
or family linage. The practice is referenced in Chinese legends, but
historians do not agree that it ever actually happened.

22. Song, *Ziyou Qu Zhongguo Caineng Kandao Weilai* [You can find the
future in China].

Chapter 5: Fooling the Emperor

1. Z. Liu, F. Yang, and M. Lu, "Tianjiang chaopiaoyu yuanlai shi zang-
kuan" [Raining money from the sky turns out to be filthy lucre],
Beijing News, September 19, 2013, http://epaper.bjnews.com.cn
/html/2013–09/19/content_466363.htm?div=-1.

2. G. Mei and Y. Li, "Lunwen maimai xingcheng wanzheng chanyelian,
09 nian guimo ji yida 10 yi" [Science paper trade formed a complete
industrial chain, reached a scale of one billion Yuan in 2009],
September 23, 2013, http://news.xinhuanet.com/politics/2013
–09/23/c_125426553.htm.

3. Jane Qiu, "Publish or Perish in China," *Nature* 463 (2010): 142–43,
http://www.nature.com/news/2010/100112/full/463142a.html.

4. Z. Wang, "Xi Jinping: Shishi chuangxin qudong buneng dengdai
guanwang xiedai" [Xi Jinping: We cannot wait, hesitate, or slacken
off our efforts in implementing innovation-driven development

strategy], October 1, 2013, http://news.xinhuanet.com/politics /2013–10/01/c_117582862.htm.

5. Alok Jha, "China Poised to Overhaul US as Biggest Publisher of Scientific Papers," *Guardian*, March 28, 2011, http:// www.theguardian.com/science/2011/mar/28/china-us-publisher -scientific-papers; Royal Society, *Knowledge, Networks and Nations: Global Scientific Collaboration in the 21st Century* (London: Royal Society, 2011).

6. Y. Cheng, "China Shows Off Scientific, Technological Achievements," September 28, 2013, http://news.xinhuanet.com/english/china /2013–09/28/c_132757994.htm.

7. X. Wang, "Zhongguo zhuanli shenqing zongliang ju shijie diyi" [The number of patent applications in China ranks top in the world], December 23, 2012, http://news.xinhuanet.com/overseas/2012 –12/23/c_124134316.htm.

8. J. Wang, "Kejibu buzhang shuju jieshuo Zhongguo keji bianhua" [Minister of science and technology uses data to explain the tech- nological changes in China], October 14, 2013, http:// news.sciencenet.cn/htmlnews/2013/10/283704.shtm.

9. J. Adams, C. King, and N. Ma, *Global Research Report China: Research and Collaboration in the New Geography of Science* (Leeds, UK: Thomson Reuters, 2009).

10. World Intellectual Property Organization, "Statistical Country Profiles: China," 2012, http://www.wipo.int/ipstats/en/statistics /country_profile/countries/cn.html.

11. "Woguo Gaoxiao Gongdu Boshi Xuewei Renshu Jinnianlai Chixu Zengzhang" [The number of PhD applicants in Chinese universities continue to rise in recent years], *China Education Online*, May 23, 2013, http://kaoyan.eol.cn/nnews_6152/20130523/t20130523 _947348.shtml.

12. L. Hu, "Jiaoyubu: Gaocengci liuxue rencai huiliulv di, boshi jinzhan 5.8%" [Ministry of Education: The return rate of top overseas talents is low, only 5.8 percent of those returned hold a doctoral degree], August 6, 2013, http://edu.gmw.cn/2013–08/06/content_8516161 .htm.

13. Ministry of Education of the PRC, *2012 Jiaoyu Tongji Shuju* [Education statistics data 2012], http://www.moe.edu.cn/publicfiles/business /htmlfiles/moe/s7567/.

14. Mark Patterson, "Open-Access Megajournals: Find Out More in Estonia," PLOS Blogs, June 20, 2011, http://blogs.plos.org/plos/2011/06/open-access-megajournals-%E2%80%93-find-out-more-in-estonia/.

15. Qiu, "Publish or Perish in China."

16. According to Jinggangshan University's 2006 guidelines encouraging scientific research.

17. Jinggangshan University, "Xuexiao jianjie" [About Jinggangshan University], October 2013, http://www.jgsu.edu.cn/xxgk/201104/t20110413_12883.htm.

18. Shanghai Jiaotong University, "Shanghai Jiaoda guanyu Hanxin shexian zaojia chuli yijian de tongbao" [Shanghai Jiaotong University's opinion on the suspected Hanxin fraud], May 12, 2006, http://tech.sina.com.cn/it/2006–05–12/1824935539.shtml.

19. N. Wen, "Guowuyuan guanyu yinfa 'Guli Ruanjian Chanye he Jicheng Dianlu Chanye Fazhan de Ruogan Zhengce' de tongzhi" [Notice of the State Council on issuing Several Policies on Encouraging the Development of the Software and Integrated Circuit Industries], June 24, 2000, http://www.mofcom.gov.cn/article/b/bf/200207/20020700031375.shtml.

20. B. Zhai, "Dalian daliang zhongxuesheng wei Gaokao jiafen Shenqing guojia zhuanli" [A large number of high school students in Dalian apply for national patents to receive bonus points in Gaokao], September 14, 2009, http://ip.people.com.cn/GB/10047024.html.

21. J. Gao and K. Wang, "Wuhan zhongxiaoxuesheng ai faming, zhuanli shenqingliang 9 Nian zeng 500 bei" [Primary and secondary school students in Wuhan love to invent, the number of patent applications increased 500 times in nine years], December 6, 2011, http://www.cnhubei.com/ctdsb/ctdsbsgk/ctdsb04/201112/t1912743.shtml.

22. C. Yu, "Wu Yingying chengwei meinu zongcai zhiqian [Before Wu Yingying became the beauty executive], Nandu Weekly Blog, http://nanduzhoukan.blog.sohu.com/28818858.html.

23. J. Xu, "Wangyou zhiyi 21 sui nvsheng fuzong jianli, dangshiren xiaofang jujue chengqing" [Internet users question the vice president title of a twenty-one-year-old female student; university refuses to clarify]. December 14, 2006, http://news.sina.com.cn/s/2006–12–14/161711791583.shtml.

24. "Fifteen Seconds of Fame: The Story of Yingying Wu and Pseudo Human Events," *High and Low,* January 2, 2007, http://cheztracey.blogspot.com/2007/01/15-seconds-of-fame-story-of-yingying_02.html.

25. J. Lu, "Who Is Making Junk Patents?" May 4, 2011, http://www.chinaipmagazine.com/en/journal-show.asp?id=690.

26. Y. Wu, China Patent No. CN1331016, China Intellectual Property Net: State Intellectual Property Office of the People's Republic of China, 2000.

27. M. Wang and J. Qu, "Zhishi chanquanju: Muqian zhuanli zhiliang hai chuzai xiangdui bijiao di shuiping" [State Intellectual Property Office of the PRC: Current patent quality is still relatively low], April 25, 2013, http://www.gov.cn/jrzg/2013–04/25/content_2390297.htm.

28. Ibid.

29. D. Prud'homme, *Dulling the Cutting-Edge: How Patent-Related Policies and Practices Hamper Innovation in China* (Shanghai: European Union Chamber of Commerce in China [European Chamber], 2012), 5.

30. Jane Qiu, "Publish or Perish in China."

31. Louisa Lim, "Plagiarism Plague Hinders China's Scientific Ambition," *NPR,* August 3, 2011, http://www.npr.org/2011/08/03/138937778/plagiarism-plague-hinders-chinas-scientific-ambition.

32. X. Jiang, "Yixue lunwen zaoyu 16 ge danwei 25 ren 6 lun lianhuan chaoxi" [Six rounds of serial plagiarism of one medical science paper by twenty-five people from sixteen organizations], March 24, 2010, http://news.sina.com.cn/c/sd/2010–03–24/052319927382.shtml.

33. Y. Wu, "Zhongyang Renmin Guangbo Diantai jiu keji lunwen shuliang yu zhiliang duiwo caifang" [China National Radio's interview with me on the quantity and quality of science papers], September 30, 2013, http://blog.sciencenet.cn/blog-1557–729177.html.

34. L. Li, X. Wu, and X. Chu, "Tongxue pingjia: Ta shi gongren de qiangren, dan juli henyuan" [Classmate judges her: She is recognized as a strong person, but aloof], December 15,

2006,   http://news.sina.com.cn/s/2006–12–15/022011793953
.shtml.

35. Prud'homme, *Dulling the Cutting-Edge*.

36. Y. Liu, K. Wen, and J. Guo, "Influence Factors Analysis of Chinese
    Patent Quality Based on the Process Management," *Scientific Research
    Management* 12 (2012): 104–9.

Chapter 6: Hell to Heaven

1. "Zheng Yefu: Zhongguo jiaoyu zhuding peiyang buchu nuojiang"
   [Zheng Yefu: Chinese education nurtures no Nobel winners],
   ThinkerBig, December 15, 2013, http://cul.qq.com/a/20131211
   /014042.htm.

2. Y. Zheng, "Cuihui chuangzaoli de Zhongguo shehui jiqi jiaoyu" [The
   Chinese society and education that destroys creativity], November
   15, 2012, http://blog.sina.com.cn/s/blog_49ccddcf0101bkjw.html.

3. Zhongguo Wang, "2012 PISA ceshi Zhejiang duo quanqiu di er"
   [Zhejiang snatches world no. 2 in PISA 2012], December 23, 2013,
   http://www.21nice.com/2013/12/1882.html.

4. Andreas Schleicher, "What We Can Learn from Educational Reform
   in China," *Huffington Post*, December 19, 2012, http://
   www.huffingtonpost.com/andreas-schleicher/educational-reform
   -in-china_b_2327908.html.

5. Andreas Schleicher, "Are the Chinese Cheating in PISA or Are We
   Cheating Ourselves?" *OECD Education Today*, December 10, 2013,
   http://oecdeducationtoday.blogspot.com/2013/12/are-chinese
   -cheating-in-pisa-or-are-we.html.

6. "On China Transcript: Education," *CNN.com*, December 17, 2013,
   http://www.cnn.com/2013/12/17/world/asia/on-china-episode
   -15-transcript/.

7. Ibid.

8. Although PISA 2009 was the first major international assessments
   with participation of students from Mainland China, students from
   other Chinese cultural circles, such as Hong Kong, Taiwan, and
   Singapore, have had a long history of outstanding performance
   in international tests. In addition, students from Mainland China
   have shown excellent performance in smaller-scale international

comparative studies since the 1980s. J. W. Stigler and J. Hiebert, *The Teaching Gap: Best Ideas from the World's Teachers for Improving Education in the Classroom* (New York: Free Press, 1999).

9. Jiang Xueqin, "Opinion: The Costs of Shanghai's Education Success Story," *CNN Opinion*, December 15, 2013, http://www.cnn.com/2013/12/04/opinion/china-education-jiang-xueqin/; Y. Zhao, *Catching Up or Leading the Way: American Education in the Age of Globalization* (Alexandria, VA: ASCD, 2009); Y. Zhao, *World Class Learners: Educating Creative and Entrepreneurial Students* (Thousand Oaks, CA: Corwin, 2012); Zhonggong Zhongyang (Central Committee of the Chinese Communist Party) and Guowuyuan (State Council), "Guanyu Shenhua Jiaoyu Tizhi Gaige Quanmian Tuijin Suzhi Jiaoyu de Jueding" [Decision to further educational systemic reform and promote quality-oriented education], 1999, http://www.chinapop.gov.cn/flfg/xgflfg/t20040326_30741.html; Zhonggong Zhongyang (Central Committee of the Chinese Communist Party) and Guowuyuan (State Council), *Guanyu Shenghua Jiaoyu Gaige Quanmian Tuijing Shuzhi Jiaoyu de Jueding* [The decision to deepen education reform and comprehensively promote quality education], 1999, http://www.edu.cn/20011114/3009834.shtml; Zhonggong Zhongyang Bangongting (Office of the Central Committee of the Chinese Communist Party) and Guowuyuan Bangongting (Office of the State Council), *Guanyu Shiying Xinxingshi Jingyibu Jiaqiang he Gaijing Zhongxiaoxue Deyu Gongzuo de Jianyi* [Suggestions for further enhancing and improving moral education in secondary and primary schools to meet the challenges of the new era] (Beijing, China: Zhonggong Zhongyang Bangongting and, Guowuyuan Bangongting, 2000).

10. Yong Zhao, *Catching Up or Leading the Way* and *World Class Learners*.

11. S. Guo and Q. Deng, "Beida maizhurou xiaoyou gengye jiang chuangye" [Peking University alumni turned pork seller sobs out his start up story: I have shamed my alma mater], April 12, 2013, http://news.sina.com.cn/s/2013-04-12/023926801066.shtml.

12. "Lu Buxuan Zhurou Yingxiao Xue" [The study of pork marketing], 2011, http://news.eastday.com/eastday/news/news/node4946/node25319/userobject1ai362899.html.

13. "Lu Buxuan jinkuang" [The recent developments of Lu Buxuan], Shengang Zaixian, October 20, 2013, http://news.szhk.com/2013 /10/20/282856962308657.html.

14. Confucius, *Lun Yu [Analects of Confucius]*, 2012, http:// ebooks.adelaide.edu.au/c/confucius/c748a/.

15. "Yu 150 Wanren Boming Guokao" [Over 1.5 million sign up for civil servant exam]," *Xin Jing Bao* [New Beijing News], 2012, http:// news.cn.yahoo.com/ypen/20121025/1384723.html.

16. Y. Shi, "Beida Lu Buxuan: Yige siyao mianzi de jiaoyu shouhaizhe" [Lu Buxuan of Peking University: A victim of the education system with a false sense of pride], April 13, 2013, http://blog.ifeng.com /article/25870773.html.

17. C. S. Chen, S.-Y. Lee, and H. W. Stevenson, "Academic Achievement and Motivation of Chinese Students: A Cross-national Perspective," in *Growing Up the Chinese Way: Chinese Child and Adolescent Development*, ed. S. Lau (Hong Kong: Chinese University Press, 1996), 69–91.

18. OECD, *Strong Performers and Successful Reformers in Education: Lessons from PISA for the United States* (Paris: OECD, 2011), 86.

19. N. D. Kristof, "China's Winning Schools?" *New York Times*, January 15, 2011, WK10, http://www.nytimes.com/2011/01/16/opinion /16kristof.html?src=me&ref=general&_r=0.

20. Sean Coughlan, "China: The World's Cleverest Country?" *BBC News*, May 8, 2012, http://www.bbc.co.uk/news/business-17585201.

21. In May 1998, Chinese president Jiang Zemin announced that the central government would invest billions of dollars in Peking University and Tsinghua University to make them world-class universities, resulting in the 985 project, which expanded later to include 39 universities. The 211 is a another project started by the Chinese government in the 1990s. It aims to develop 100 leading universities in the twenty-first century. A total of 112 universities are included. In 2011, the minister of education announced that no more universities would be added to these two projects.

22. L. Liu and W. Shi, "Jiedu jiaoyubu youguan 'Xianding 985, 211 Gaoxiao Biyesheng Jiuye Zhaoping' jinling" [Interpretation of the Ministry of Education's ban on "only recruiting graduates from

universities in the 985 and 211 projects"], May 4, 2013, http://news.xinhuanet.com/2013–05/04/c_115635472.htm.

23. Renming Wang, "Huhehaoteshi Shiyan Zhongxue "Huojianban" Xuesheng Tiaolou Zhuizong" [Student commits suicide at Hohhot Experimental School], 2012, http://edu.people.com.cn/n/2013/0123/c79457–20303521.html.

24. W. Ma, "Anhui Xuexiao Kaoshi An Mingci Pai Zuowei Shifou Qishi Chasheng Ying Zhiyi" [Schools in Anhui assign seats based on test scores, practice questioned for discrimination], *Zhongguang Wang* [China Radio Network], November 16, 2011, http://edu.ifeng.com/news/detail_2011_11/16/10695716_0.shtml?_from_ralated.

25. S. Lin and Q. Wang, "Zhao'an Nancheng Zhongxue Yi Qishi Chasheng, Jing Paiming Kaoqiang Xuesheng Wuchang Buke" [Nancheng Middle School in Zhao'an suspected of discriminating against poor students; only top ranked offered free tutoring], November 22, 2011, http://fj.sina.com.cn/xm/news/sz/2011–11–22/085827064.html.

26. G. Liang, "Qishi Chasheng Jiushi Peiyang Chouhen" [Discrimination against "poor" students cultivates hatred], 2011, http://opinion.people.com.cn/GB/16202580.html.

27. D. Yang, "PISA Shanghai diyi de sikao" [Thoughts on Shanghai ranking no. 1 in PISA], December 31, 2013, http://yangdongping.blog.sohu.com/300129534.html.

28. "China Enters 'Testing-Free' Zone: The New Ten Commandments of Education Reform," blog entry by Yong Zhao, August 22, 2013, http://zhaolearning.com/2013/08/22/china-enters-%E2%80%9Ctesting-free%E2%80%9D-zone-the-new-ten-commandments-of-education-reform/.

29. Jiang Xueqin, "Opinion: The Costs of Shanghai's Education Success Story," *CNN Opinion,* December 15, 2013, http://www.cnn.com/2013/12/04/opinion/china-education-jiang-xueqin/.

30. K.-M. Cheng, "Shanghai: How a Big City in a Developing Country Leaped to the Head of the Class," in *Surpassing Shanghai: An Agenda for American Education Built on the World's Leading Systems,* ed. M. S. Tucker (Cambridge, MA: Harvard Education Press, 2011), 34.

31. Xueqin, "Opinion: The Costs of Shanghai's Education Success Story."

32. M. Tucker, ed., *Surpassing Shanghai: An Agenda for American Education Built on the World's Leading Systems* (Cambridge, MA: Harvard Education Press, 2011), 174–75.

33. "Ditch Testing (Part 4): Test Security Measures in China," blog entry by Yong Zhao, July 17, 2011, http://zhaolearning.com/2011/07/17 /ditch-testing-part-4-test-security-measures-in-china/.

34. Malcolm Moore, "Riot after Chinese Teachers Try to Stop Pupils Cheating," *Telegraph*, June 20, 2013, http://www.telegraph.co.uk /news/worldnews/asia/china/10132391/Riot-after-Chinese -teachers-try-to-stop-pupils-cheating.html.

35. Zhao, *World Class Learners.*

36. H. M. Levin, "More Than Just Test Scores," *Prospects: The Quarterly Review of Comparative Education* 42 (2012): 269–84; G. Brunello and M. Schlotter, *The Effect of Non Cognitive Skills and Personality Traits on Labour Market Outcomes* (Munich: European Expert Network on Economics of Education, 2010).

37. The tuition is determined based on students' exam scores from the previous year. The higher a student's scores, the lower his or her tuition.

38. Xuan Chen, "Anhui Maotan Chang Zhongxue Cheng Gaokao Shengdi" [Anhui's Maotan Chang High School becomes the mecca of college entrance exam], *China Youth*, September 18, 2013, http:// news.xinhuanet.com/politics/2013–09/18/c_125407252_2.

39. Y. Wang, "Maotanchang Zhongxue: Yazhou zuida gaokao jiqi, tong-wang tiantang de diyu" [Maotanchang High School: The biggest Gaokao factory in Asia, a hell like path to heaven], July 26, 2013, http://learning.sohu.com/20130726/n382658649.shtml.

40. Ibid.

41. Ibid.

42. W. Chen, " 'Gaokaozhen' shenhua" [The myth of "Gaokao Town"], June 14, 2013, http://newsweek.inewsweek.cn/magazine.php ?id=6641&page=3.

43. Guojia Jiaowei (National Education Commission), "Guanyu Dangqian Jiji Tuijin Zhongxiaoxue Shishi Shuzhi Jiaoyu de Ruogan

Yijian" [Several suggestions for the promotion of quality education in secondary and elementary schools], Beijing, 1997, http://xhongcom.diy.myrice.com/page1/fagui/newpage8.htm.

Chapter 7: The Witch That Cannot Be Killed

1. X. Liu, Y. Lu, X. Guo, and Q. Huo, "Cai Rongsheng ban jiahuzhao chuangguan chuguo bei danghuo, Renda huoyou xin dongzuo" [Cai Rongsheng caught fleeing the country with fake passport, Renmin University may take new actions], November 30, 2013, http://news.sohu.com/20131130/n391050540.shtml.

2. To minimize room for tampering with college admission, the Chinese government has established an elaborate system. Universities do not directly receive student applications. Instead, all student files are controlled by a separate government agency. Students indicate their preferences for universities to the agency. The agency, typically at the provincial level, determines cut scores for different tiers of universities and controls how many student applications a university can review based on a formula. The standard formula gives each university 20 percent more applications than the actual number of students each university is allowed to admit. For example, a university that is allowed to admit 100 students receives 120 applications to review. All students who indicated the university as their first choice are ranked based on their *gaokao* scores. If there are more than 120 on the list, the agency picks only the top 120. If there are fewer than 120, the university reviews whatever number they receive and waits for those who picked it as their second choice and were rejected by their first choice.

3. Jianguang Yin, "Shiyi Sui Fuerdai Shang Renda Shi Cai Rongsheng Yigeren Zai Zhandou Ma" [Could Cai Rongsheng have admitted an 11-year-old child of the wealthy to the People's University by himself?], *People's Daily Forum*, December 16, 2013, http://opinion.people.com.cn/n/2013/1216/c1003–23849061.html.

4. Ministry of Education of the PRC, "Jiaoyubu Bangongting guanyu jinyibu jiaqiang gaoxiao zizhu xuanba luqu gaige shidian guanli gongzuo de tongzhi" [Notice of the General Office of the Ministry of Education on further enforcing the University Autonomous

Enrollment Reform Pilot Administration], December 30, 2013, http://www.moe.edu.cn/publicfiles/business/htmlfiles/moe/s3110/201312/161571.html.

5. Renmin Wang, " 'Wenhua da geming' yu jiaoyu wutuobang" ["Cultural Revolution" and education utopia], February 3, 2010, http://book.ifeng.com/special/49nianhoudaxue/201002/0203_9420_1536319_1.shtml.

6. D. Yang, "Wenhuadageming yu Jiaoyu Wutuobang" [Cultural Revolution and education utopia]. October 20, 2006, http://theory.people.com.cn/GB/68294/72286/72288/4939387.html.

7. M. Zedong, *"Mao Zhuxi Lun Jiaoyu Geming" [Chairman Mao on educational revolution]* (Beijing: Renming Chubangshe, 1967), 54.

8. Ibid., 68.

9. S. Li, "Dajia Doulai Guanxin Gaoxiao Zhaosheng" [Let's all pay attention to college admissions], *People's Daily*, September 21, 1970.

10. D. Yang, *Zhongguo Jiaoyu Gongping de Lixiang yu Xianshi [The ideal and reality of education equity in China]*. (Beijing: Peking University Press, 2006).

11. Three-Good Students is an honor bestowed on students who have demonstrated excellence in three areas: academic, moral, and physical health. The awards are given at school, district, provincial, and national levels. Only a limited of number of students receive them each year. L. Luo, "Historical Evolvement and Introspection of Extra Credit Policy in the College Entrance Examination," *Kaoshi Yanjiu* [Examinations research] 4, no. 3 (2008): 36–48.

12. C. Mao, "Chongqing: 31 Ming Jia Minzu Sheng Quxiao Gaokao Jiafeng Diaocha" [Chongqing: Investigation of the invalidation of bonus points for 31 fake ethnic minority students in the college entrance exam], *Xinhua Net Chongqing Channel*, June 29 2009, http://www.gs.xinhuanet.com/jiaodianwt/2009–06/29/content_16939767.htm.

13. X. Wu, X. Wan, and B. Li, "Gaokao Jiafeng Zhengce Cunzai Zhidu Loudong, Jiafeng Baosong Cheng Chanye" [Exploitation of loopholes in bonus points awarding policy in the college entrance exam becomes an industry], *China Youth*, June 16, 2006, http://www.china.com.cn/chinese/news/1243970.htm.

14. Jiaoyu Bu (Ministry of Education), "Guanyu jinyibu zuohao xiaoxue shengru chuzhong mianshi jiujin ruxue gongzuo de shishi yijian" [Suggestions for further improving the implementation of policies regarding transition from primary school to middle school without exams], *Xinhua Net*, January 26, 2014, http://news.xinhuanet.com /edu/2014–01/26/c_119141269.htm.

15. B. Zhou, "Jiaoting bianxiang 'xiao sheng chu' ruxue kaoshi" [Stop the alternative exams for advancing from primary to secondary schools], *Chengdu Daily*, April 23, 2010, http://news.163 .com/10/0423/04/64U6H31C00014AED.html.

16. Y. Ye, "Xiaoshengchu jibian" [Distorted middle school matriculation], 21st Century Education Research Institute. September 28, 2013, http://www.21cedu.org/index.php?m=content&c=index&a=s how&catid=124&id=3320&page=4.

17. X. Li, "Yinxing he bianxiang kaoshi cheng xiaoshengchu zhuliu, jiujin ruxue buzhi suozhong" [Hidden and alternative exams become mainstream for secondary school matriculation. Policies regarding residence-based enrollment ended without effect], *China Youth*, December 11, 2013, http://news.xinhuanet.com/edu/2013 –12/11/c_125838505.htm.

18. D. Jiao, "Jinling shi ruhe shixiao de" [How the ban lost its effectiveness], *China Weekly*, September 17, 2013, http://www.chinaweekly.cn /bencandy.php?fid=63&id=6847.

19. Ministry of Education, "Jiaoyubu guanyu jianqing zhongxiao xuexiao xuesheng guozhong fudan de zhishi" [Ministry of Education's instructions to reduce the excessive burden on primary and secondary school students], July 1, 1955, http://blog.sina.com.cn/s /blog_576b52430102e3mc.html.

20. "China Enters 'Testing-Free' Zone: The New Ten Commandments of Education Reform," blog entry by Yong Zhao, August 22, 2013, http://zhaolearning.com/2013/08/22/china-enters-%E2%80% 9Ctesting-free%E2%80%9D-zone-the-new-ten-commandments-of -education-reform/.

21. P. Li, "Zuiyan jianfuling zhuanyi fudan dao xiaowai, fudaoban huobao jiaofu maiduanhuo" [The strictest decree to alleviate burden has transferred the burden after school, tutoring market exuberant

and teaching materials sold out], *Guangming Wang*, March 25, 2013, http://edu.gmw.cn/2013–03/25/content_7158015_3.htm.

22. "Nash Equilibrium," *Investopedia*, http://www.investopedia.com /terms/n/nash-equilibrium.asp.

23. G. Hardin, "The Tragedy of the Commons," *Science* 62 (1968): 1243–48.

24. Ibid.

Chapter 8: The Naked Emperor

1. Saga Ringmar, "Here's the Truth about Shanghai Schools: They're Terrible," *Guardian*, December 28, 2013, http://www.theguardian .com/commentisfree/2013/dec/28/shanghai-china-schools -terrible-not-ideal.

2. Organization for Economic and Cooperative Development, *Ready to Learn: Students Engagement, Drive, and Self-Beliefs* (Paris: OECD, 2013), 15.

3. Ibid.

4. Organization for Economic and Cooperative Development, *Strong Performers and Successful Reformers in Education: Lessons from PISA for the United States* (Paris: OECD, 2011).

5. M. S. Tucker, *Standing on the Shoulders of Giants: An American Agenda for Education Reform* (Washington, DC: National Center Education and the Economy, 2011); M. Tucker, ed., *Surpassing Shanghai: An Agenda for American Education Built on the World's Leading Systems* (Cambridge, MA: Harvard Education Press, 2011).

6. M. Tucker, *Chinese Lessons: Shanghai's Rise to the Top of the PISA League Tables* (Washington, DC: National Center on Education and the Economy, 2014).

7. W. Stewart, "Is PISA Fundamentally Flawed?" December 3, 2013, http://www.tes.co.uk/article.aspx?storycode=6344672.

8. S. Kreiner and K. B. Christensen, "Analyses of Model Fit and Robustness. A New Look at the PISA Scaling Model Underlying Ranking of Countries According to Reading Literacy," *Psychometrika* 72 (2014): 210–31; Stewart, "Is PISA Fundamentally Flawed?"

9. S. T. Hopmann, Gertrude Brinek, and M. Retzl, eds., *PISA zufolge PISA—PISA According to PISA* (Berlin: Lit Verlag, 2007).

10. Ibid., 10.

11. Ibid., 12–13.

12. Andreas Schleicher, "Attacks on Pisa Are Entirely Unjustified," *TESconnect*, March 11, 2014, http://www.tes.co.uk/article.aspx ?storycode=6345213.

13. "Pisa 2012 Major Flaw Exposed," *Pace N. Ireland Education Weblog*, March 13, 2014, https://paceni.wordpress.com/2013/12/01 /pisa-2012-major-flaw-exposed/.

14. Stewart, "Is PISA Fundamentally Flawed?"

15. "Pisa 2012 Major Flaw Exposed."

16. S. Sjøberg, "PISA: Politics, Fundamental Problems and Intriguing Results." *Recherches en Education* 14 (2012): 7, http://www.recherches -en-education.net/spip.php?article140.

17. Ibid., 3.

18. H. M. Levin, "More Than Just Test Scores." *Prospects: The Quarterly Review of Comparative Education* 42 (2012): 269–84.

19. Andreas Schleicher, "Are the Chinese Cheating in PISA or Are We Cheating Ourselves?" *OECD Education Today*, December 10, 2013, http://oecdeducationtoday.blogspot.com/2013/12/are-chinese -cheating-in-pisa-or-are-we.html.

20. Tom Loveless, "PISA's China Problem Continues: A Response to Schleicher, Zhang, and Tucker," *Brookings*, January 8, 2014, http:// www.brookings.edu/blogs/brown-center-chalkboard/posts/2014 /01/08-shanghai-pisa-loveless.

21. Schleicher, "Are the Chinese Cheating in PISA or Are We Cheating Ourselves?"

22. All data from OECD, *Ready to Learn*.

23. Ibid., 62.

24. According to *Democracy Index 2012*, an annual ranking of 165 coun- tries' state of democracy produced by the Economist Intelligence Unit, an international research group. Economist Intelligence Unit, *Democracy Index 2012: Democracy at a Standstill* (London: Economist Intelligence Unit, 2013).

25. D. Baumrind, "Effects of Authoritative Parental Control on Child Behavior," *Child Development* 37 (1966): 887–907.

26. Based on aggregated data from OECD, *Ready to Learn*, 304.

27. Based on aggregated data from ibid., 310.

28. Stephen R. McIntyre, "The Works of Mencius," http://nothingistic
.org/library/mencius/mencius48.html.

29. H. W. Stevenson and J. W. Stigler, *The Learning Gap: Why Our Schools Are Failing and What We Can Learn from Japanese and Chinese Education* (New York: Simon & Schuster, 2006), 95.

30. Alix Spiegel, "Struggle for Smarts? How Eastern and Western Cultures Tackle Learning," *NPR*, 2012, http://www.npr.org/blogs /health/2012/11/12/164793058/struggle-for-smarts-how-eastern -and-western-cultures-tackle-learning.

31. Kai-ming Cheng, "Shanghai: How a Big City in a Developing Country Leaped to the Head of the Class," in *Surpassing Shanghai: An Agenda for American Education Built on the World's Leading Systems*, edited by Marc S. Tucker (Cambridge, MA: Harvard Education Press, 2011), 21–50; Robert Compton, "Two Million Minutes: About the Film," 2008, http://2mminutes.com/about.html; Alix Spiegel, "Struggle for Smarts? How Eastern and Western Cultures Tackle Learning," *NPR*, 2012, http://www.npr.org/blogs/health/2012/11/12 /164793058/struggle-for-smarts-how-eastern-and-western-cultures -tackle-learning.

32. A. Chua, *Battle Hymn of the Tiger Mother* (New York: Penguin Group, 2011).

33. "Xiao baiyou, suoyi, beida xiongmei" [Ergo, brothers and sisters admitted to Peking University], *Shanghai Sanlian Shudian*, 2011; L. Li, "Dajin Beida? Langba de 'chenggong' hennan fuzhi" [Beat them into Peking University? The "success" of Wolf Dad difficult to repli-cate], *Sina*, November 2, 2011, http://star.news.sohu.com/s2011 /langba/.

34. A. Miller, *For Your Own Good: Hidden Cruelty in Child-Rearing and the Roots of Violence* (New York: Farrar, Straus & Giroux, 1980), 58–59.

35. D. Gribble, *A Really Good School* (London: Seven-Ply Yarns, 2001).

36. D. Gribble, "Poisonous Pedagogy," http://www.authoritarian schooling.co.uk/index.php/poisonous-pedagogy.

37. Y. Zhao, *World Class Learners: Educating Creative and Entrepreneurial Students* (Thousand Oaks, CA: Corwin, 2012).

38. Ibid.

39. Tucker, *Chinese Lessons.*

40. G. Zhang and Y. Zhao, "Achievement Gap in China," in *Closing the Achievement Gap from an International Perspective: Transforming STEM for Effective Education,* ed. J. V. Clark (New York: Springer, 2014), 217–228.

41. I wrote about this in Zhao, *World Class Learners.*

42. D. Farrell and A. J. Grant, *China's Looming Talent Shortage* (New York: McKinsey and Company, 2005).

BIBLIOGRAPHY

Adams, J., C. King, and N. Ma. *Global Research Report China: Research and Collaboration in the New Geography of Science.* Leads, UK: Thomson Reuters, 2009.

Angang, H., H. Linlin, and C. Zhixiao. "China's Economic Growth and Poverty Reduction (1978–2002)." Paper presented at A Tale of Two Giants: India's and China's Experience with Reform and Growth, meeting of the International Monetary Fund and National Council of Applied Economic Research (India), New Delhi, November 14–16, 2003.

Backhouse, E., and J. O. P. Blan. *Annals and Memoirs of the Court of Peking.* Boston: Houghton Mifflin, 1914.

Baumrind, D. "Effects of Authoritative Parental Control on Child Behavior." *Child Development* 37 (1996): 887–907.

Belk, R. W., and N. Zhou. "Learning to Want Things." *Advances in Consumer Research* 14 (1987): 478–81.

Bieler, S. *"Patriots" or "Traitors"? A History of American-Educated Chinese Students.* New York: East Gate, 2004.

Brunello, G., and M. Schlotter. *The Effect of Non Cognitive Skills and Personality Traits on Labour Market Outcomes.* Munich: European Expert Network on Economics of Education, 2010.

Chen, C.-S., S.-Y. Lee, and H. W. Stevenson. "Academic Achievement and Motivation of Chinese Students: A Cross-National Perspective." In *Growing Up the Chinese Way: Chinese Child and Adolescent Development,* edited by S. Lau, 69–91. Hong Kong: Chinese University Press, 1996.

Chen, G., and C. Wu. *Xiaogangcun de Gushi* [Stories of Xiaogang Village]. Beijing: Huawen Chubanshe, 2009.

Cheng, K.-M. *Shanghai: How a Big City in a Developing Country Leaped to the Head of the Class.* In *Surpassing Shanghai: An Agenda for American Education Built on the World's Leading Systems,* edited by M. S. Tucker, 21–50. Cambridge, MA: Harvard Education Press, 2011.

Chua, A. *Battle Hymn of the Tiger Mother.* New York: Penguin Group, 2011.

Confucius. *Lun Yu* [Analects of Confucius]. Adelaide, Australia: University of Adelaide, 2012. http://ebooks.adelaide.edu.au/c/confucius/c748a/.

Connor, S. "US Science Chief Warns: 'China Will Eat Our Lunch.'" *Independent,* February 20, 2011.

Davis, A. R. "The Character of a Chinese Scholar-Official as Illustrated by the Life and Poetry of T'ao Yuan-Ming." *Arts: The Journal of the Sydney University Arts Association* 1, no. 1 (1958): 37–46.

Deng, X. *Deng Xiaoping Wenxuan Disanjuan* [Selected works of Xiaoping Deng]. Beijing: Renming Chubanshe, 1993.

Economist Intelligence Unit. *Democracy Index 2012: Democracy at a Standstill.* London: Economist Intelligence Unit, 2013.

Editorial Team of Biography of Wang Zhen. *Wang Zhen Zhuan* [Biography of Wang Zhen]. Beijing: Dangdai Zhongguo Chubanshe, 2001.

Elliott, M. "China Takes on the World." *Time,* January 11, 2007. http://www.time.com/time/magazine/article/0,9171,1576831,00.html#ixzz2Rl3Z2myN.

Fairbank, J. K., & M. Goldman. *China: A New History.* Cambridge, MA: Harvard University Press, 2001.

Farrell, D., and A. J. Grant. *China's Looming Talent Shortage.* New York: McKinsey and Company, 2005.

Fishman, T. C. *China Inc.: How the Rise of the Next Superpower Challenges America and the World.* New York: Scribner, 2005.

Gribble, D. *A Really Good School.* London: Seven-Ply Yarns, 2001.

Hardin, G. "The Tragedy of the Commons." *Science* 62, no. 3859 (1968): 1243–48.

Hopmann, S. T., and Gertrude Brinek. *PISA according to PISA.* Berlin: Lit Verlag, 2007.

Hu, W. *Dizhi de Zhongjie* [The end of imperial rule]. Beijing: Zhongguo Dangdai Chubanshe, 2011.

Kreiner, S., and K. B. Christensen. "Analyses of Model Fit and Robustness: A New Look at the PISA Scaling Model Underlying Ranking of Countries According to Reading Literacy." *Psychometrika*, June 2013, 1–22.

Kristof, N. D. "China's Winning Schools?" *New York Times*, January 15, 2011. http://www.nytimes.com/2011/01/16/opinion/16kristof .html?src=me&ref=general&_r=0.

Kurlantzick, J. *Democracy in Retreat: The Revolt of the Middle Class and the Worldwide Decline of Representative Government.* New Haven, CT: Yale University Press, 2013.

Leibovitz, L., and M. Miller. *Fortunate Sons: The 120 Chinese Boys Who Came to America, Went to School, and Revolutionized an Ancient Civilization.* New York: Norton, 2012.

Levin, H. M. "More Than Just Test Scores." *Prospects: The Quarterly Review of Comparative Education* 42 (2012): 269–84.

Li, G. "Feichu Keju Bainian" [A century after the demolition of Keju]. 2005. http://news.xinhuanet.com/comments/2005–08/29 /content_3415631.htm.

Li, Z. "Dajia Doulai Guanxin Gaoxiao Zhaosheng" [Let's all pay attention to college admissions]. *People's Daily*, September 21, 1970.

Liang, G. *Qishi chasheng jiushi peiyang chouhen* [Discrimination against "poor" students cultivates hatred]. 2011. http://opinion.people.com .cn/GB/16202580.html.

Lin, J. Y. "Needham Puzzle, Weber Question and China's Miracle: Long Term Performance since the Sung Dynasty." Paper presented at the World Economic Performance: Past, Present and Future—Long Term Performance and Prospects of Australia and Major Asian Economies, 2006. http://www.uq.edu.au/economics/cepa/docs /seminar/papers-nov2006/Lin-Paper.pdf.

Lin, S., and Q. Wang. "Zhao'an Nancheng Zhongxue Yi Qishi Chasheng, Jing Paiming Kaoqiang Xuesheng Wuchang Buke" [Nancheng Middle School in Zhao'an suspected of discriminating against poor students; only top-ranked offered free tutoring]. November 22,

2011. http://fj.sina.com.cn/xm/news/sz/2011–11–22/085827064 .html.

Litten, J. A. *American-Educated Chinese Students and Their Impact on U.S.-China Relations*. Williamsburg, VA: College of William and Mary, 2009.

Liu, Y., K. Wen, and J. Guo. "Influence Factors Analysis of Chinese Patent Quality Based on the Process Management." *Keyan Guanli* [Scientific research management] 12 (2012): 104–9, 141.

Luo, L. "Historical Evolvement and Introspection of Extra Credit Policy in the College Entrance Examination." *Kaoshi Yanjiu* [Examinations research], 4, no. 3 (2008): 36–48.

Ma, L. *Jiaofeng: Gaige Kaifang Sici Dazhenglun Qingliji* [Thirty years of battle: Personal experiences with the four great debates of reform and opening-up]. Nanjing, China: Jiangsu Reming Chubanshe, 2008.

Ma, M. "Anhui Xuexiao Kaoshi An Mingci Pai Zuowei Shifou Qishi Chasheng Ying Zhiyi" [Schools in Anhui assign seats based on test scores, practice questioned for discrimination]. *Zhongguang Wang* [China Radio Network], November 16, 2011. http://edu.ifeng.com /news/detail_2011_11/16/10695716_0.shtml?_from_ralated.

Mao, Z. *Mao Zhuxi Lun Jiaoyu Geming* [Chairman Mao on educational revolution]. Beijing: Renming Chubangshe, 1967.

Miller, A. *For Your Own Good: Hidden Cruelty in Child-Rearing and the Roots of Violence*. New York: Farrar, Straus & Giroux, 1980.

New, S. C. "Chinaland: Across the Sea." *Exonian*, May 29, 1880.

Nichols, S. L., and D. C. Berliner. *Collateral Damage: How High-Stakes Testing Corrupts America's Schools*. Cambridge, MA: Harvard Education Press, 2007.

Organization for Economic Cooperation and Development. *Strong Performers and Successful Reformers in Education: Lessons from PISA for the United States*. Paris: OECD, 2011.

Organization for Economic Cooperation and Development. *Ready to Learn: Students Engagement, Drive, and Self-Beliefs*. Paris: OECD, 2013.

Pak, H. B. *China and the West: Myths and Realities in History*. Leiden, Netherlands: E. J. Brill, 1974.

Prud'homme, D. *Dulling the Cutting-Edge: How Patent-Related Policies and Practices Hamper Innovation in China*. Shanghai: European Union Chamber of Commerce in China, 2012.

Pugach, N. "Embarrassed Monarchist: Frank J. Goodnow and Constitutional Development in China: 1913–1915." *Pacific Historical Review* 42, no. 4 (1973): 499–517.

Qian, G., and J. Hu. *Daqing Liumei Youtong Ji* [Chinese Educational Mission students]. Beijing: Dangdai, 2010.

Ramo, J. C. *The Beijing Consensus.* London: Foreign Policy Center, 2004.

Ravitch, D. *The Death and Life of the Great American School System: How Testing and Choice Are Undermining Education.* New York: Basic Books, 2010.

Renming Wang. "Huhehaoteshi Shiyan Zhongxue 'Huojianban' Xuesheng Tiaolou Zhuizong" [Student commits suicide at Hohhot Experimental School]. 2013. http://edu.people.com.cn/n/2013 /0123/c79457-20303521.html.

Rhoads, E. J. M. *Stepping Forth into the World: The Chinese Educational Mission to the United States, 1872–81.* Hong Kong: Hong Kong University Press, 2011.

Rowbotham, A. H. "Voltaire, Sinophile." *PMLA* 47 (1932): 1050–65.

Royal Society. *Knowledge, Networks and Nations: Global Scientific Collaboration in the 21st Century.* London, UK: Royal Society, 2011.

Sjøberg, S. "PISA: Politics, Fundamental Problems and Intriguing Results." *Recherches en Education* 14 (2012): 1–21. http://www.recherches -en-education.net/spip.php?article140.

Song, L. "Ziyou Qu Zhongguo Caineng Kangdao Weilai" [You can find the future in China]. *Hong Qi Wen Gao,* 2013.

Song, P. "Nian Guangjiu: Shui ye Wufa Daiti de Geshi Jingji Biaobeng Renwu" [Nian Guangjiu: An irreplaceable specimen of private enter-prises]. *Chutian Xinwen Guangbo.* China.com.cn. 2008.

Spence, J. D. *The Search for Modern China.* New York: Norton, 1990.

Stevenson, H. W., and J. W. Stigler. *The Learning Gap: Why Our Schools Are Failing and What We Can Learn from Japanese and Chinese Education.* New York: Simon & Schuster, 2006.

Stewart, W. "Is Pisa Fundamentally Flawed?" December 3, 2013. http:// www.tes.co.uk/article.aspx?storycode=6344672.

Stigler, J. W., and J. Hiebert. *The Teaching Gap: Best Ideas from the World's Teachers for Improving Education in the Classroom.* New York: Free Press, 1999.

Stross, R. E. *Bulls in the China Shop and Other Sino-American Business Encounters.* New York: Pantheon, 1990.

Su, X., and L. Wang. *Heshang* [River Elegy]. Beijing: Xiandai Chubanshe, 1988.

Tian, Z. *Zhongguo Jiaoyushi Yanjiu: Jindai Fengjuan* [Study of Chinese education history: Modern period]. Shanghai, China: East China Normal University Press, 2009.

Tucker, M. S. *Standing on the Shoulders of Giants: An American Agenda for Education Reform.* Washington, DC: National Center Education and the Economy, 2011.

Tucker, M. ed. *Surpassing Shanghai: An Agenda for American Education Built on the World's Leading Systems.* Cambridge, MA: Harvard Education Press, 2011.

Tucker, M. *Chinese Lessons: Shanghai's Rise to the Top of the PISA League Tables.* Washington, DC: National Center on Education and the Economy, 2014.

Winston, K. "Advisors to Ruler—or, What the Kennedy School of Government Can Learn from Chinese Scholar-Officials, and Vice Versa." Working paper, Harvard Kennedy School of Government, Cambridge, MA, 2005.

Woo, T. T. "Chinese Educational Commission." *Hartford Daily Courant,* April 1, 1880. http://www.colebrookhistoricalsociety.org/PDF%20 Images/Chinese%20Educational%20Mission.pdf.

Wu, X. *Jidang Sanshi Nian* [Thirty years of reform]. Beijing: Zhongxin Chubanshe, 2008.

Wu, Y. China Patent No. CN1331016. China Intellectual Property Net: State Intellectual Property Office of the People's Republic of China, 2000.

Xu, Q. *Siying Jingji Shi Zengme Huode "Zhunshengzheng" de* [How private economy received its legal status]. April 30, 2007. http://theory.people .com.cn/GB/49154/49155/5689522.html.

Yang, D. "Wenhuadageming yu Jiaoyu Wutuobang" [Cultural revolution and education utopia]. October 20, 2006. http://theory.people.com .cn/GB/68294/72286/72288/4939387.html.

Yang, D. *Zhongguo Jiaoyu Gongping de Lixiang yu Xianshi* [The ideal and reality of education equity in China]. Beijing: Peking University Press, 2006.

"Yu 150 Wanren Boming Guokao" [Over 1.5 million sign up for civil servant exam]. *Xin Jing Bao* [New Beijing News], 2012. http://news.cn.yahoo.com/ypen/20121025/1384723.html.

Yung, W. *My Life in China and America.* Stratford, NH: Ayer Company, 2000. First published 1909 by Henry Holt.

Zhang, G., and Y. Zhao. "Achievement Gap in China." In *Closing the Achievement Gap from an International Perspective: Transforming STEM for Effective Education,* edited by J. V. Clark, 217–28. New York: Springer, 2014.

Zhang, X. "Woguo Getihu Shoupo 4000 Wan Hu" [Getihu in China exceeds 40 million for the first time]. February 16, 2013. http://finance.chinanews.com/cj/2013/02–16/4564431.shtml.

Zhao, Y. *Catching Up or Leading the Way: American Education in the Age of Globalization.* Alexandria, VA: ASCD, 2009.

Zhao, Y. *World Class Learners: Educating Creative and Entrepreneurial Students.* Thousand Oaks, CA: Corwin, 2012.

Zhen, H. *Zhenzheng ba Chuanxin Qudong Fazhan Zhanlue Luodao Shichu* [Truly realize the innovation-driven development strategy]. *Liaowang Zhoukang* [Outlook weekly], 2013(30).

Zhonggong Zhongyang (Central Committee of the Chinese Communist Party) and Guowuyuan (State Council). Guanyu Shenhua Jiaoyu Tizhi Gaige Quanmian Tuijin Suzhi Jiaoyu de Jueding [Decision to further educational systemic reform and promote quality-oriented education]. 1999. http://www.chinapop.gov.cn/flfg/xgflfg /t20040326_30741.html.

Zhonggong Zhongyang (Central Committee of the Chinese Communist Party) and Guowuyuan (State Council). "Guanyu Shenghua Jiaoyu Gaige Quanmian Tuijing Shuzhi Jiaoyu de Jueding" [The decision to deepen education reform and comprehensively promote quality education]. 1999. http://www.edu.cn/20011114/3009834.shtml.

Zhonggong Zhongyang Bangongting (Office of the Central Committee of the Chinese Communist Party) and Guowuyuan Bangongting (Office of the State Council). *Guanyu Shiying Xinxingshi Jingyibu Jiaqiang he Gaijing Zhongxiaoxue Deyu Gongzuo de Jianyi* [Suggestions for further enhancing and improving moral education in secondary and primary schools to meet the challenges of the new era]. Beijing, China: Zhonggong Zhongyang Bangongting and Guowuyuan Bangongting, 2000.

INDEX

A

Academic burden: Chinese
Ministry of Education
attempts to reduce, 151–154;
Cultural Revolution's
reduction of, 151, 154;
prisoner's dilemma of
reforming, 156; ten actions
for Chinese schools to take
to reduce, 152–153

Acta Crystallographica Section E
journal, 101–102

Airbus, 65

American education: cheating
scandals of the, 1–3; cultural
assumption that achievement
comes from innate ability,
180; emulating Chinese
education as potential
disaster for, 167; high-stakes
testing and accountability
system driving cheating in, 3;
mistaken commitment to
authoritarian education by,

7–8; "Sputnik moment"
response to Chinese PISA
results by, 21; tragedy of
continued support for
high-stakes testing, 3–4;
tragedy of loss of values
traditionally celebrated by, 5;
why we must not emulate
Shanghai, 184–189. *See also*
Education systems

American Educational Research
Association, 1

American Federation of Teachers,
4

American Heritage Dictionary,
108

America's National
Superintendent of the Year
(2009), 1

Amherst College, 77

Annapolis Naval Academy, 76

Anti-Spiritual Pollution campaign
(1983) [PRC], 86

Apple, 65